MW01050187

# JEWELRY

Nancy N. Schiffer

4880 Lower Valley Road, Atglen, PA 19310 USA

**Revised 3rd Edition**

## Nature preserved

Diamond brooch and pendant designed as two birds in flight with a leaf garland suspended from their beaks, $3500-5000. / Stick pin of a flying bird set with turquoise and a rose diamond beak, $500-650. / Victorian gold articulated snake necklace, the engraved head with emerald, diamond, rose diamond and gem decoration, the engraved tail with four stone emerald line, with alternative side or mouthpiece clasp, $5000-6800. / Turquoise cameo depicting a classical female profile, mounted as a brooch with diamond entwined twin serpent surround, $3500-4000. / Emerald and diamond lizard brooch with gem-set eyes, $2500-3000. / Wasp brooch with two colors of gold, black enamel and rose diamond, $960-1280. / Articulated snake necklace, the head pavé-set with turquoise and ruby eyes, $2250-2500. / Diamond brooch modeled as a drop shaped cluster surmounted by a diamond pavé-set butterfly, $1600-1800. / Reverse crystal intaglio of a dog, mounted as a brooch, $320-480. Christie's London.

Revised price guide: 2001
Library of Congress Card Number: 2001086080
Copyright © 1996 & 2001 by Schiffer Publishing, Ltd.
"Schiffer," "Schiffer Publishing Ltd. & Design," and the "Design of pen and ink well" are registered trademarks of Schiffer Publishing, Ltd.
Typeset in Lydian BT/ZapfHumnst Dm BT
ISBN: 0-7643-1373-8
Printed in China       1 2 3 4

## Acknowledgments

My grateful thanks are extended to all the people who helped me play with this project, particularly those knowledgeable jewelry lovers at the following collections: Anne's Arts, Chestnut Hill, Philadelphia; Armour-Winston, Ltd., London; Bill and Dee Battle; Bel Arte, London; Bentley & Co, Ltd., London; Bizarre Bazaar, New York; N. Bloom & Son Antiques, Ltd., London; Linnet Bolduc; W. & F.C. Bonham & Sons, Ltd., London; Christie Manson & Woods, Ltd., London; Christie's East, New York; Cobra & Bellamy, London; Norman Crider Antiques, New York; Sandy DeMaio Antique Jewelry, Bryn Mawr, Pa; Fior Collection, London; Jackie Fleishman, Black Angus Mall, Adamstown, Pa; Diana Foley, London; Elizabeth Goodson, Moderne, London; Beebe Hopper; John Joseph, London; Clive Kandel, Magnificent Costume Jewelry, New York; Muriel Karasik, New York; M. Klein, Philadelphia; Lucia Lambert, London; McPeabody's Antiques; Phillips Auction, London; Leonard D. Prins, Strafford, Pa; Terry Rodgers, New York; E. & J. Rothstein Antiques, West Chester, Pa; Malvina Solomon, New York; Sotheby's Auction, London; Wartski, London.

## Contents

### Fantasy friends

An 18k. gold owl brooch perched on a diamond line branch, the body with guiloché enamel decoration and pearl eyes, by Boucheron, $4850-5500. / Amusing dog brooch with black and white enamel eyes, $775-875. / Diamond pavé-set pink panther brooch with gem-set eyes and black enamel nose by Kutchinsky, $4250-4850. / Diamond-set brooch designed as a skiing duck, $3500-4500. / Diamond and demantoid garnet climbing frog brooch, $950-1200. / Demantoid garnet, green garnet and diamond frog brooch, $1200-1400. / Rose diamond and emerald grasshopper brooch with polychrome enamel, maker's mark SP, $3000-4000. / 18k. gold duck brooch with diamond-set bow tie and gem-set eye, $1500-1800. Christie's London.

### Sentimental journey

These Victorian brooches convey heartfelt sentiments. Art Nouveau brooch of an enamel plaque of four children's faces enhanced by colorfully enameled flowers and leaves, circa 1900. / Heart and ribbon brooch-pendant with a pear-shaped emerald and circular emerald surrounded by pavé diamonds. / Bicycle brooch with rotating wheels set with rubies and diamonds and an enameled seat and handle bars, mounted in yellow gold. Christie's East, New York. Left to right, $2250-3250, Special, $4800-6500.

### Set in silver

Marcasite and enamel decoration brings out the details of these brooches designed in a variety of figural themes, circa 1940s. Fior. $95-275 each.

# Fun with Jewelry

Come with us on an enjoyable romp through the jewelry box. The journey reaches back to our ancestors and comes right up to the moment we pick up this book. Take your time, it's not a race. In your leisure, then, remember Grandma's favorite brooch, and the stories told of Auntie and Uncle's heirlooms cherished for a special event and the places they visited.

Our path can be a hop here and there as pages are turned, or it can be a straight stick-to-the-trail adventure from start to finish because your imagination navigates your way.

The delightful jewelry collected here is arranged by the images from nature it replicates. Beginning in the sea, the *Swimmers* lead off. Fish, frogs and serpents propel through many design styles of historical importance to contemporary delight. The chapters evolve to dry land where *Blossoms* greet you along the track and wind through gardens of floral jewelry from single flowers to bowers of buds. The insects are noticed next, *Crawlers and Low Flyers* whose busy work in the garden is so essential, and fascinating to many who enjoy wearing bug jewelry. Further along are the *Beasts*, highly specialized animals from the wild savages of safaris to their domesticated cousins of the suburbs and cities. The *People* who "civilize" this environment greet you in all the peculiar costumes suited to their occupations, native customs, or activities of pleasure. Finally, the *High Flyers* zoom across the pages, the birds whose freedom to be themselves is so envied, for they see all the lowly activity below and yet maintain their inbred habits regardless of the building or tearing down of other devils.

And so we wish you a tremendously enjoyable time.

**Popular innovations**
Figural designs such as these by Kenneth Jay Lane circa 1965 to 1975 have greatly contributed to the popularity of costume jewelry. Because they are a great deal of fun to wear, women have supported the growth of the costume jewelry industry in the 20th century. Joan Rothstein Toborowsky of E. & J. Rothstein Antiques. Necklace $750-900, bee $250-325, rose $250-350, horse $250-350, earrings $175-225.

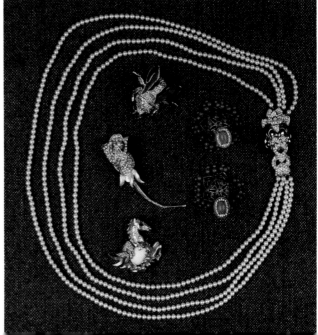

**Victorian treasure**
A bangle bracelet formed by a double headed serpent of gold, blue enamel, half-pears and cabochon gems, $1800-2250. / A link bracelet of gold, half-pearls and blue enamel, with a central locket with applied diamond and gem fly, $3800-4800. / Bar brooch with a blue enamel and a half coiled snake suspending a matching heart shaped locket pendant, $450-550. / A diamond, pearl and gem-set bee brooch with a detachable fitting, $1250-1550. / An articulated snake necklace, the blue enamel head with rose diamond decoration and gem-set eyes, $4500-6000. Christie's London.

*Opposite page:*
**Playful creatures**
Gold bar pin with playing kittens set with a rose diamond and pearl, $425-575. / Polychrome enameled flying pheasant brooch with central cabochon garnet, $250-300. / Gold and polychrome enamel kingfisher brooch, $275-375. / Diamond pavé-set dove mounted as a brooch with pearl and diamond terminals, $800-900. / Rose diamond pavé set chick and wishbone brooch, $700-850. / Garnet and cabochon garnet stag beetle brooch, $300-400. / Rose diamond and gem dragonfly brooch with green enameled body, $600-750. / Bloodhound head stick pin with ruby eye, $275-425. / Rose diamond twin monkey bar brooch, $450-500. / A twin

duckling brooch, $95-145./ Gold dog brooch with blue enamel eyes, $175-250. / Gold and chrysoprase rabbit brooch with gem-set eyes, $195-245. / Rose diamond dog's head stick pin, $225-275. / Rose diamond snipe head stick pin with gem-set eye, $275-425./ Pair of lovebirds in gold set with pearls and gems, $500-650. / Diamond running fox brooch, $1750-1950. / Continental, diamond, ruby and turquoise openwork owl brooch, $375-500. / Diamond, rose diamond and red and green enameled pheasant brooch, $375-475. / Rose diamond and two-color gold turtle brooch with gem-set eye, $275-375. / An oval openwork poly-chrome enameled brooch depicting a spaniel against a brass background, $350-450. Christie's, London.

# *Swimmers*

*Opposite page:*
**Winter memories**
Edwardian diamond, pearl and platinum snowflake brooch, circa 1900, $750-1000. / Victorian diamond star brooch, circa 1870, $4000-5000. / Three diamond and gem-set Christmas charms, circa 1988, $600-650 each. / Victorian diamond running horse brooch, circa 1860, $2250-2500. / Gold and diamond reindeer brooch, circa 1960, $850-975. / Eskimo brooch, French, circa 1960s, $1600-1850. / Gold Christmas tree brooch set with gems, circa 1980, $1250-1500. N. Bloom & Sons.

**Beach memories**
Wonderful variety of ocean life captured in costume jewelry, none marked. $45-150 each. Beebe Hopper.

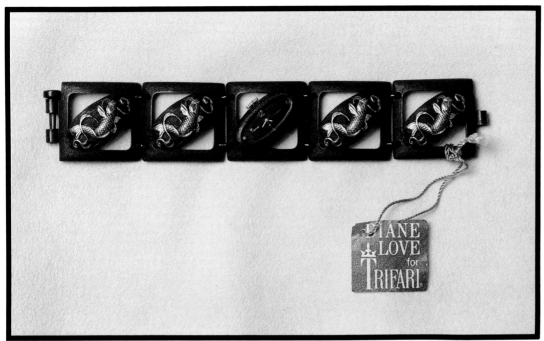

**Time for fishing**
Wristwatch with link bracelet band, each molded metal link with an oriental style fish design by Diane Love for Trifari, 1972. Clive Kandel. $500-750.

**We're all moving**
Scarf pins for the adventure-bound. Sailfish of platinum set with 30 diamonds by J. F. Calwell. / Submarine of 14k. gold and platinum, 13 diamonds, seven rubies and six olivines, circa 1900-1910. / Antique automobile of 14k. gold and platinum with 15 diamond and two ruby headlights. Private collection through Leonard D. Prins. Left to right, $3200-3500, $2750-3250, $2750-3250.

**A fishing expedition**
Flowerhead brooch or pendant of carved citrine and 18k. gold, circa 1930s. / Victorian stork with green garnets and diamond, 1880s. / Fish brooch of 15k. gold, circa 1880s. N. Bloom & Son. Top to bottom, $8250-9500, $6250-6850, $525-650.

**Swimming carp**
Chinese enameled fish of linked segments mounted as a
pendant. $1250-1850.

**Of far-reaching concern**
Gold octopus grasping a fish brooch with diamonds,
probably Italian, circa 1965. N. Bloom & Son. $4250-4650.

**Beached tuna**
Plastic habitat with palm trees and
elephant by Stanislaw Kucharczyk. /
Fish brooch of molded plastic. /
Alligator brooch of molded and
textured plastic, circa 1950. Cobra &
Bellamy Palms $1500-1800, alligator
$175-250, fish $175-250.

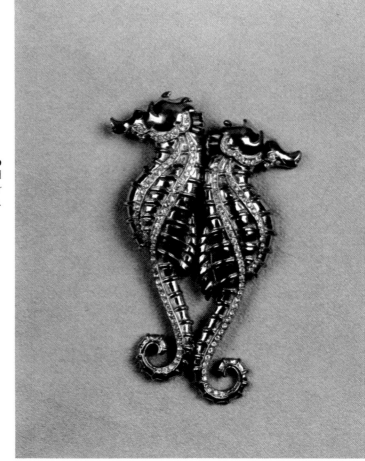

**Monsters of the deep**
Gigantic pair of costume seahorses, a full 4″ long, by Coro Duette. Norman Crider Antiques. $750-1000.

**Nautical nifties**
Each of these costume jewelry pins moves, trembles and delights observers with their use of motion to extend the image. None are marked. Norman Crider Antiques. $150-250 each.

**Neptune's stallion**
Seahorse brooch of green finished metal set with glass cabochons, by Chanel, circa 1960. Cobra & Bellamy. $750-1000.

**Pearls from the sea**
Bracelet of cast fish motifs joined with faux pearls and glass beads designed by Mitchell Maer for Christian Dior, circa 1954. Fior. $500-700.

**Seashells**
Belt buckles in cast metal by Mimi diN; one shell, 1973, $85-135; shell group, 1976, $95-145. Beebe Hopper.

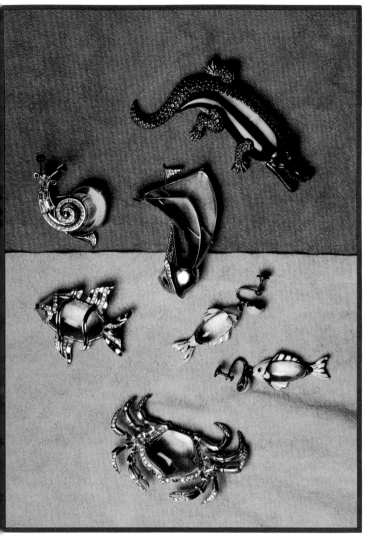

**Sterling swimmers**
Fish and seahorse design in a sterling silver brooch by Beau. Linnet Bolduc. $100-150.

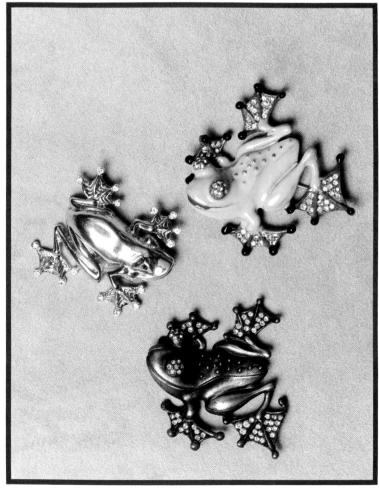

**Clear winners**
Carved Lucite dominates these sea life designs. Alligator brooch with no makers mark, circa 1940, $500-750. / Snail brooch by Trifari circa 1950, $500-750./ Sailboat brooch by Trifari, circa 1944, $500-750. / Fish brooch by Coro, circa 1950, $500-750. / Pair of fish earrings by Coro, circa 1940, $250-300. / Crab brooch by Trifari, circa 1944, $500-750. Clive Kandel.

**Family resemblance**
Jewelry designs seems to migrate to other ponds. Copper frog brooch marked by Isser Singer & Son, 989 6th Ave., N.Y.C., circa 1938, $300-500. / Yellow and green enamel frog brooch marked Chanel, circa 1938, $700-900. / Shiny golden frog brooch marked Corocraft, circa 1945, $100-150. Clive Kandel.

**Amphibians take note**
Clear Lucite forms the central element of these "jelly belly" designs. The lobster and carved turtle are unmarked, the frog is marked sterling, and all others are by Trifari, circa 1944. Joan Rothstein Toborowsky of E. & J. Rothstein Antiques. Left to right: top, $250-500, $275-375, (crab) $450-600, (turtle) $225-300, $250-350; bottom, (lizard) $300-450, (turtle) $225-275.

*Opposite page:*
**Clear water creatures**
Lucite molded into charming designs of marine life including four brooches and two pendants, circa 1945, none marked. Elsa Rothstein of E. & J. Rothstein Antiques. Fish bowl, $150-250, fish pendant (bottom left) $100-150, all brooches $150-200 each.

**Creatures of the deep**
Sterling silver and Lucite in fish designs, three with clear rhine-stones and red eyes by Trifari, others unmarked. Joan Rothstein Toborowsky of E. & J. Rothstein Antiques. $350-600 each.

**The croaking contest**

Gold frog brooch with green bellystone by ART, circa 1970, $100-150. / Green enameled frog brooch with rhinestone leaves by Corocraft, circa 1944, $250-350. / Purple enameled frog with colored glass warts by Kenneth Jay Lane, circa 1968, $250-350. / White enameled frog brooch by Kenneth Jay Lane, circa 1968, $125-175. / Green enameled frog brooch with red eyes by HAR, circa 1960, $150-225. / Sweater pins of green enameled frog and lily pad joined by a double chain by Trifari, circa 1972, $125-150. / Lucite and sterling silver frog circa 1945, $250-350. / Sweater pins of gold frogs with rhinestones joined by a chain by Nettie Rosenstein, circa 1944, $200-250. Clive Kandel.

**The serpent pit**
Lively matching set of jewelry with a serpent theme made with enameled and mesh metal and carved opaque and clear rhinestones by HAR, circa 1955. Clive Kandel. $1250-1750 set.

**Sealife duets**
Five sterling silver Coro Duette pairs including green frogs with matching earrings, sea horses, turtles and fish. Norman Crider Antiques. Large frogs with small frog earrings $350-450/set, seahorses $250-325, green turtles $275-350, clear turtles $300-450, fish $325-475.

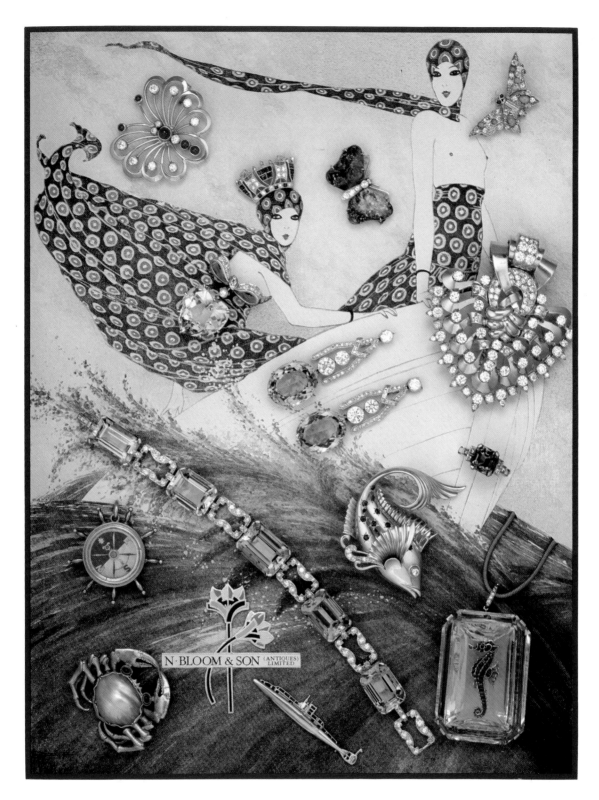

**A fishing trip**

Butterfly brooch of 18k. gold with cabochon rubies and diamonds, circa 1950s, $2250-2500. / Naval crown brooch of 18k. white gold and platinum with diamonds and sapphires, $1500-1750. / Butterfly brooch of black opal and diamonds, $3200-3500. / Butterfly brooch of gold and silver with diamonds and turquoise, Victorian, $2500-3000. / Heart-shaped aquamarine with diamond bow top, $5000-6000. Edwardian earrings of aquamarine and diamonds set in white gold, $1800-2000. / Brooch of 18k. gold and diamonds by Van Cleef and Arpels New York, circa 1950s, $18,000-24,000. / Ring of blue zircon and diamonds in platinum and 18k. gold, $1000-1250. / Fish brooch of 18k. gold, sapphires and diamonds, French, 1950s, $3000-3500. / Ship's wheel compass pendant of 15k. gold, Victorian, $500-700. / Crab brooch of 15k. gold with baroque pearl body and banded agate eyes, Victorian, $1500-1750. / Submarine brooch of 9k. gold, 1930, $300-350. / Bracelet of aquamarine and diamonds in 18k. white gold, 1920s, $18,000-20,000. / Aquamarine mystery pendant enclosing a buff-top sapphire and emerald sea horse, with platinum, sapphire and emerald girdle mount, Cartier, Paris, $30,000-40,000. N. Bloom & Son.

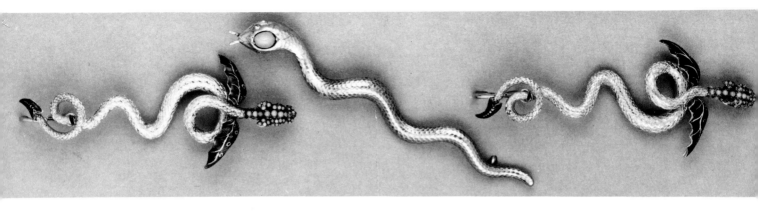

### Golden serpents
Pair of earrings designed as winged serpents in textured gold, enamel and pearls, English, circa 1840, $750-1250. / Snake brooch of hammered gold and pearl, circa 1900, $1250-1750. Wartski.

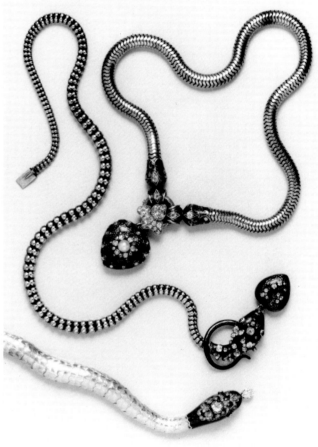

### Cold water delicacy
Lobster brooch of copper by Rebajez. Muriel Karasik. $475-600.

### Snake chains
Necklace of gold Brazilian linked chain with royal blue enamel scroll motifs and diamonds supporting a blue guilloché enamel heart shaped locket with half-pearls and diamonds circa 1870, $2200-2500. / Necklace designed as a serpent with gold scale-like linked chain, the head and tail with blue guilloché enamel and diamonds, the eyes of carbuncles, supporting a similar heart-shaped pendant, circa 1845, $3000-3500. / Bracelet designed as a coiled serpent with scale-like links, guilloché enamel, and diamonds, circa 1840, $3000-3500. Sotheby's London.

# Blossoms

**Tropical marvels**
Marcasite and colored enamels decorate the orchid and other floral
designs of these unsigned brooches, Fior. $200-500 each.

**In the winner's circle**
Spectacular flowerhead with pavé petals by Christian Dior, 1959, $200-325. / Green ribbon and pavé rhinestones by Ciner, $125-225. / Trefoil leaf of pavé stones by Polcini, $150-200. / Two red blossoms with pearl centers by Ciner, $250-350. / Golden feather by Christian Dior 1958, $200-250. / Openwork pavé leaf by Christian Dior, 1959, $175-250. / Red, white and blue clustered flower by Ciner, $175-225. Fior.

**Nostalgic nosegays**
Delicate silver bouquets are accented with tiny colored glass stones to create unmarked brooches from the 1950s. Fior. $125-200 each.

**Genius in motion**
The petals of this brooch can be folded open or closed making its
ingenious design, by Warner, a great deal of fun to play with, circa
1950. Beebe Hopper. $200-300.

**Antique enamels**
Each of these brooches was made with superior craftsmanship around the turn of the century. Lavender enamel poppy
brooch on 14k. gold, American, $1600-1800. / Plique-à-
jour enamel vine brooch of 18k. gold, French, $3850-4500.
/ Pansy enamel brooch of 14k. gold with a pearl, $1500-
1750. / Clover brooch of 18k. gold and enamel with
diamonds, $750-900. / Art Nouveau poppy brooch of 14k.
gold, a diamond and pearls, $2000-2500. / Primrose brooch
of 18k. gold and a diamond, $1250-1500. / Oxalis leaf
brooch of enamel on 18k. gold and a diamond, $1500-
1800. / *Ixia veridiflora* brooch of 18k. gold and diamonds. N.
Bloom & Son.

**Forget me not**
Enamel and 18k. gold brooch with a
diamond and pearl accents. John
Joseph. $1250-1500.

**Coventry gardens**
Each of these brooches, and the several matching earrings, was made for Sarah Coventry Jewelry in the 1950s and 1960s to be sold at Home Parties by enterprising neighbors. Beebe Hopper. Brooches $25-60 each, sets $75-95.

### Irresistible mechanicals
Movable parts on each of these brooches create fascination that few can resist. The two on the left are, surprisingly, unmarked, $200-300 each. The center and top right brooches were made by Les Bernard, Inc., $200-300 each. The tulip is a locket, shown in two views below, $200-300. Norman Crider Antiques.

**Trembling plants**
Plant forms all, but a diverse group of unmarked designs suggest the endless variety of tremblers that can be found in the costume jewelry group. Norman Crider Antiques. $175-350 each.

**A festival of flowers**
Eight different floral designs in clips by Coro Duette. Norman Crider Antiques. $250-450 each.

**Over the moon about these**
Copies of moonstones are featured in these costume duet clips. Art Deco style with blue moonstones by Trifari Clipmates. / Scrolled design with blue moonstones by Criner. / Two half oval designs marked Patented. / Opaque pink and aqua carved stones which are unmarked. / Dark blue floral groups by Coro Duette. Pink moonstones by Coro Duette. / Pink rhinestones with single moonstones, sterling silver, by Coro Duette. / Pink enamel roses by Coro Duette. / Aqua shell design by Coro Duette, circa 1955. Norman Crider Antiqes. $150-300 each.

**Magnolia time**
White enameled metal was shaped into this cool magnolia blossom by Robert Originals in the 1960s. Beebe Hopper. $100-150.

**Barely alighting**
A filigree butterfly trembles above this bouquet of shell and pearl-like plastic blossoms on an unmarked pierced metal brooch, circa 1945. Norman Crider Antiques. $125-150.

**Flower power**
These three brooches of dynamic floral designs by Carven are each
accented with enameled leaves. Fior. $225-350 each.

**Simply marvelous**
Earrings and a fine pearl drop brooch all designed by Marvella. Beebe Hopper. Floral earrings $30-50, pearl set $75-100.

**Fruit and flowers**
Lucite and silver joined to create these special brooches in the early 1940s: orchid blossom by Trifari, $350-450; cornucopia with enamels by Corocraft, $325-400; bouquet which was made also in several different colors, $350-450; and lily of the valley by Trifari, $300-375. Clive Kandel.

**Cultivated taste**
Trifari made these costume pieces of great detail circa 1940: a windmill, $250-350; an apple, $175-225; and a sprig of fruit (who can name it?), $225-325; all with shaded enamels and rhinestones. Clive Kandel

**Gardening tools**
The red plastic necklace is a charming relic from the 1940s, $275-350. / Green molded plastic forms a floral cluster brooch of morning glory blossoms, $125-200. / An unusual floral bouquet brooch wraps a printed paper design in clear Lucite which is signed in ink on the back 100 by B. + L.M. Canada, $125-175. Bess Goodson.

**Land of fruit and nuts**
Discontent as a mere edible variety, one brooch has taken on a unique and happy personification, none marked. Beebe Hopper. $35-85 each.

**Soft shades**
Delicate leaf and blossom shapes of molded plastics in shaded tones of pink comprise this bead necklace from the 1940s. Beebe Hopper. $275-375.

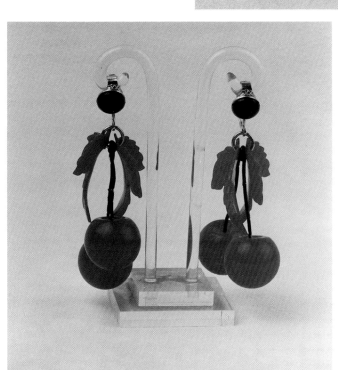

**Cheerful ear bobs**
Bright red cherries of molded plastic dangle from the ear clips to create these silly decorations which are practically irresistible. Cobra & Bellamy. $200-350.

**Solitaire simplicity**
Dynamic floral designs are highlighted with rhinestones on these brooches, circa 1939. The purple iris is by Trifari, $350-425. / The golden flower has a movable petal position, $150-225. / The tiger lily and rose are unmarked, $375-450 and $350-425 respectively. Clive Kandel.

**Stars of the past**
Pink and blue cabochon stones, replicating star sapphires, and rhinestones accents are used in a pleasing bouquet design in this brooch by Reja from the 1950s. Beebe Hopper. $200-275.

**Fantastic plastic**
Fruit designs lend themselves to the varied colors of plastic molded in the 1940s. Bess Goodson. $95-300 each.

**Queen Anne's lace**
Iridescent stones focus color into this shimmering design inspired by the summer wildflower common to upland meadows. The unmarked brooch and earrings make a beautiful set. Beebe Hopper. $145-195/set.

**It's the berries!**
Red plastic cherries decorate a link bracelet and double necklace from the 1940s. Now who can wear these and keep a sober face? McPeabody's Antiques. $400-500/set.

**They light up your life**
Christmas tree brooches including battery operated designs at the top (by Corocraft) and left which illuminate, and movable designs at the center and right. Have a merry one! Norman Crider Antiques. $75-135 each.

**Christmas glitter**
Decorated Christmas trees abound in varied designs, this group
showing earring and brooches which are unmarked. Beebe
Hopper. Earrings $25-45/pair, brooches $45-100 each.

**Pearls and glass in harmony**
Beads and carefully constructed floral clusters have been combined to create a brooch (with Andre and "Rosalinda" tags), $175-225; necklace, $325-400; bead bracelet, $175-250; and hinged bangle bracelet, $150-200, all by Coro, mid-1950s. Fior.

*Opposite page:*
**Sheer imagination**
This unusual necklace and earring set by Trifari conveys the daring fantasy of a water fountain which its designer achieved by combining silver leaves and chains with blue glass in a graduated garland design with a long tassel, circa 1962. E. & J. Rothstein Antiques. $800-1000.

**Roses of gold**
Pendant and earrings of multi-colored gold and pearls in a rose design within a frame, late 19th century. N. Bloom & Son. $4500-5500.

**Bracelet set**
The Coro Duette clip and matching bracelet have blossoms mounted on springs to tremble with every move. They always attract attention, circa 1945. Norman Crider Antiques. $800-1250.

### Renewed interest
The designs for the golden bar pin and bracelet were made by Coro in about 1939, to be renewed for their Vendome line in about 1965 for the black bracelet. Clive Kandel. $1200-1500 for gold set, $300-500 for black bracelet.

### It's a symphony
Set of costume jewelry with blending designs of floral motifs which complement, but do not repeat, one another. Bracelet, double brooch and earrings made by Coro Duette. Norman Crider Antiques. $700-900/set.

**Get set and go**
Matching flower heads of beautifully detailed design and colored stones are mounted as a set of necklace, duet clips and bracelet by Coro. Norman Crider Antiques. $700-900.

**Necklace set**
Three duet brooches designed to match this necklace of beautifully sculpted and set rhinestones, each with trembling flowerheads. The designer is unknown, circa 1945. Norman Crider Antiques. Necklace $700-900, duettes $300-450 each.

**Newfangled bangle**
Ingenious design helped create these hinged bangle bracelets mounted with duet clips. Neither is signed by its maker, but the one with the red stones is marked Sterling. Norman Crider Antiques. $750-1250 each.

**All linked up**
Sterling silver bracelet of floral panels linked together, made by Hobé, circa 1945. M. Klein. $650-850.

**The blue orchid**
Bracelet of 18k. gold, blue enamel, French cut clear stone and pearls, late 19th century. Terry Rodgers. $1500-2000.

**Swaying in the breeze**
Four fine amethyst and 14k. gold are combined in a scrolling floral design by Krementz which captures the image of a frond bending in a gentle wind. N. Bloom & Son. $400-650.

**Wild roses**
Copper and brass are used together to form the flowerheads and leaves of this lovely brooch by Trifari which is highlighted with rhinestones, from the 1940s. N. Bloom & Son. $800-1000.

**An American beauty**
Superb bracelet of exquisite workmanship and design in a rose motif, circa 1939, unmarked. Clive Kandel. $700-900.

**Memories of a distant time**

Floral spray clip brooch of colored sapphires and rubies set in gold, $2500-3000. / Serpent necklace of articulated gold with a cabochon garnet head and rose diamond eyes, 19th century, $1000-1200. / Victorian opal nine-stone half hoop hinged bracelet with diamonds, dated 1895, $1200-1600. / Bracelet of woven rope design and cabochon sapphire and diamond cluster, $5000-6000. / Pendant of swag design with a citrine and three diamonds, $550-750. / Flower spray brooch of gold with diamonds and rubies, $1250-1750. / Bow brooch and gold ropes set with diamonds, $1250-1750. Christies, London.

*Top:* **A new variety**
Gold textured wires create flowers of a new variety with diamond pistols and leaves to create a pair of brooches and earrings. N. Bloom & Son. $2000-2500 each.

*Bottom left:* **Water lilies**
American Art Nouveau gold brooch with pink enameled water lilies, a pair of swan figures, and diamond accents, circa 1900. Sandy DeMaio. $795-1000.

*Bottom right:* **French daisies**
Enameled daisies clustered at the closure of a 14k. gold wire bracelet made in France. Anne's Arts. $600-800.

*Opposite page:* **Flights of fancy**
Flowerhead brooch and earrings of gold by Cartier, 1940s, $4500-5500/set. / Butterfly brooch in plique-à-jour enamel with diamonds, circa 1880, $2000-2500. / Ladybug pins of red enamel by Cartier, 1930s, $2250-2500/set. N. Bloom & Son.

**Blooming wonders**
Spectacular flower brooch with movable petals in rose diamonds, Burma rubies, turquoise, and sapphires by John Rubel Co., New York, 1940s, no value available. Rose brooch with moveable woven petals in diamonds, Burma rubies and emeralds by Parmentier, Paris 1940s, $5000-7000. N. Bloom & Sons.

**Arranged for pleasure**
Basket of flowers brooch set with cluster of rubies, sapphires emeralds, demantoid garnets and diamonds, $2250-2500. / Vase of flowers set with clusters and collets of rubies, emeralds, sapphires and diamonds, $3000-3500. Phillips Auction.

**Colored and engraved**
Duet clips with engraved colored stones and clear pavé rhinestones in a style sometimes called "fruit salad." The top duet by Coro Duette, $450-600. / The next two duets by Trifari, $375-550 and $400-600 respectively. / The bottom duette marked Patented, $375-475. Norman Crider Antiques.

**Fruit and flowers**
Natural pink pearls and diamonds are arranged in gold to produce an outstanding brooch of Art Nouveau inspiration with plique-à-jour and translucent enamels by Marcus & Co., New York, circa 1900. N. Bloom & Son. No value available.

**Paired elegance**
Four Coro Duette clips with pierced designs of distinctive elegant workmanship. Norman Crider Antiques. $150-350 each.

**The accent on red**
Five Coro Duette clips of golden tone and floral designs all accented with red stones. Norman Crider Antiques. $175-400 each.

**A bunch of fun**
Purple grape clusters with bow knots form a Coro Duette
clip which tastefully complements the necklace of matching
graduated beads. Norman Crider Antiques. $275-400.

**Classy, clever clips**
Heart-shaped outline surrounding a floral design by Trifari Clip-Mates, $250-325. / Golden metal with clear baguette sprays by Coro Duette, $175-250. / Six clear big stones on an unmarked duet clip, $125-175. / Tulip designs in gold washed sterling clips by Coro Duette, $250-425. / Small scrolled designs in an unmarked duet group, $175-225. Norman Crider Antiques.

**Floral duets**
Fine detail is evident in the openwork bouquets with the blue stones by Trifari Clip-Mates, $225-275. / Patented duet clips with enamel decoration, $200-300. / Coro Duettes in a clear (top right) and a red variation (bottom left) of a double-flowerhead design, $250-350 each. / Sterling silver design with floral motif in oval topaz colored glass, $350-450. / Coro Duette clip of gold bouquets with red stones and faux pearls, $300-400. Norman Crider Antiques.

**Clustered beauties**
A cluster of fireflies form a trembling brooch by Boucher, $375-500, above a bold flowerhead trembler in clear stones with golden and silvered metal, unsigned, $175-275. A large rhinestone cluster trembles, too, on a necklace entirely constructed from glass stones, also unsigned, $250-350. A large rhinestone cluster trembles, too, on a necklace entirely constructed from glass stones, also unsigned, $600-800. Norman Crider Antiques.

**Pretty posy**
The floral designs of five duet clips by Coro Duette are joined by the
bar brooch/ clips, the clips with the turquoise and gold stones, and
the floral clips with green enameled leaves which are not marked by
their makers. Norman Crider Antiques. Duette clips $275-400, bar
brooch $145-195, turquoise clips $200-250, floral clips $200-300.

*Opposite page:*
**Double the pleasure**
Nine different and beautiful Coro Duette clips, all double
flowerheads. Norman Crider Antiques. $200-400 each.

### Bow knots and flowers
Trifari Clip-Mate in a shoe bow design, $225-375. / Coro Duette openwork ribbon bow, $275-375. / Sterling silver ribbon and bouquet design, $325-450. / Two leaves by Coro Duette, $200-300. / Sterling silver large double bouquets, $375-475. / Two small bouquets with curled ribbons, $250-350. / Two thistles by Coro Duette, $175-250. / Double swirl by Coro Duette, $150-200. Norman Crider Antiques.

### The last leaf
Amethyst colored stones and an openwork design create the last word in down to earth beauty, simply a leaf and no more, by Hollycraft. $125-165.

### Trembling petals
The design shimmers as brown and blue glass is mounted on delicately balanced wires with tear-shaped drops in this magnificent brooch by Schreiner of New York, 4 1/2" long. Norman Crider Antiques.

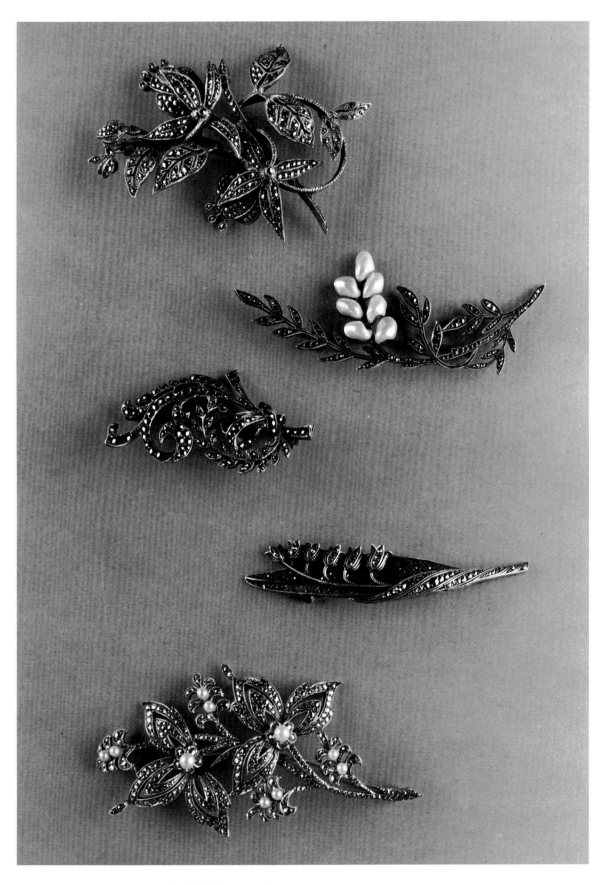

**Delights in marcasite**
Five floral brooches of silver set with marcasites, none
marked. Malvina Solomon. $150-400 each.

**Frozen in time**
Iris blossom of carved amethyst and diamonds mounted a brooch of significant splendor. Bonham's Auction. $2250-2500.

**Purple passion**
Opaque and translucent purple stones are combined in this delicate brooch by star. Beebe Hopper. $95-145.

**Sunflower**
Strong design gives this single sunflower head of sterling silver a commanding presence. Jackie Fleischman. $300-500.

**Sterling bouquet**
Silver wrought into a bouquet brooch of twisting flowers and leaves, early 20th century. Jackie Fleischman. $225-350.

**A posy for a lady**
Carved lapis lazuli, rose quartz and frosted crystal from the flowers of a special posy brooch set with diamond clusters. Bonham's Auction. $1850-2250.

**Fit for an Empress**
Enormous ruby and diamond laurel branch hair or bodice ornament which really did belong to the French Empress Josephine (1763-1814), French, circa 1805. It is now in the Victoria and Albert Museum. Wartski. No value available.

**Filigree formality**
The fine detail of these sterling silver filigree brooches, four with the same design but differently colored enamel panels, includes marcasite accents, none marked. Fior. $350-550 each.

**More than an Easter basket**
Colored diamonds, not eggs, fill this basket of delights. The stones are cut in many shapes so their variety becomes a source of considerable interest, circa 1935. Wartski. No value available.

*Opposite page:*
**Enduring flower arrangement**
Fine craftsmanship of golden and silvered petals, is exhibited on the elaborate floral pendant of this necklace by Miriam Haskell, 1940s. Bel Arte. $1250-1500.

**Swinging flower baskets**
Exquisite earrings of considerable distinction with emeralds, diamonds and pearls are designed as flower baskets suspended from collet-set graduated diamond ropes. N. Bloom & Son. No value available.

**Spray of summer blooms**
Elegant Victorian spray brooch of rubies and diamonds united by superior design and craftsmanship. N. Bloom & Son. $5000-6000.

**For the Emperor's table**
Exotic flowers in a distinctive bowl mounted as a brooch. The footed bowl of pavé diamonds with black onyx, sapphire beads, and a square cut ruby filled with flowers composed of ruby, emerald and sapphire blossoms with diamond pavé petals. Christie's, New York. $5000-6000.

**A budding beauty**
French Art Nouveau brooch of 18k. gold with pastel enamel and diamonds. Sandy DeMaio. $1500-1750.

**Garland in diamonds**
English mid-Victorian diamond necklace of floral motifs in a lovely repeating pattern. Armour-Winston Ltd. No value available.

**Inspired by roses**
A softly colored pink glass stone is encircled by silver rose blooms and leaves to create this brooch by Hobé from about 1945. Joan Rothstein Toborowsky of E. & J. Rothstein Antiques. $400-600.

**A good vintage**
Diamonds and gold are blended to create this unusual necklace and earrings of exceptional grape design from the 19th century. Wartski. No value available.

**Framed and ready to go**
A magnificent brooch of pierced silver set with marcasites is designed as a trio of flowerheads within an ornate frame. M. Klein. $250-325.

**Bring her flowers**
These little nosegays should do the job. Bouquets of emerald, diamond, ruby and sapphire flowers mounted as an important brooch and earrings. Phillips Auction. $7500-8500.

**Ice of a different climate**
Three trailing drops of graduated diamonds swing like icicles from the late 19th century English floral brooch. Wartski. $10,000-12,000.

**Georgian grace**
An 18th century floral spray diamond brooch of exquisite workmanship incorporating stones of varying shapes. Truly fascinating. Wartski. No value available.

**Surrounded**
The five pendant floral designs of this diamond necklace are joined by a delicately linked garland of leaf and plant motifs, circa 1920. Wartski. No value available.

**And it moves, too**
18th century English pavé diamond floral brooch with the large flowerhead mounted *en tremblant*. Wartski. $9000-11,000.

**Edwardian charm**
As a revival of English 18th century taste, Edwardian style sought to bring back some of the opulence of the previous century, as witnessed in this diamond floral brooch of the late 19th century. Wartski. $7500-9000.

# Crawlers and Low Flyers

**Striking resemblance**
Gold wasp brooch with black enamel, diamonds and gem-set eyes.
Christie's, London. $500-600.

**What's the buzz?**
This silver moth has his antenna set to catch all the news that
he can not see with his own bug eyes. Jackie Fleischman.
$1200-1500.

**In the footsteps of the ancients**
19th century Etruscan style brooch and pendant earrings of gold
with mosaic depicting a fly. Christie's, London. $2500-3000.

**A good news carrier**
Late 19th century brooch in the design of a flying
moth, set with a mother-of-pearl body and ruby,
sapphire and rose-cut diamond wings. Phillips
Auction. $1500-1750.

### Coming in for a closer look

Large Edwardian butterfly of platinum wires and fancy colored diamonds, no price available. / Victorian gold chain necklace tiara with graduated fringe drops of diamonds and pearls, $10,000-12,000. / Three platinum charms by Cartier, circa 1930: a nutcracker with diamond, sapphire and emerald, $500-750; / a cocktail shaker in diamond and gems, $1000-1200; / a skater set with diamonds, $1000-1200. / Bar brooch of 9k. gold with a replica of the Eiffel Tower and pearls, $400-500. / The R101 Airship brooch in 9k. gold, circa 1930, $550-650. N. Bloom & Son.

**Out of the garden**
Four naturalistic brooches of enamel washed metal and
rhinestones by Marcel Boucher, circa 1941, including a
praying mantis; a grasshopper; a hummingbird; and a fanciful
swallow, $500-800 each. Clive Kandel.

## Something's buzzing
Two sterling silver enameled brooch and earring sets designed as blue fireflies, $275-350, and yellow honeybees, $225-300. Norman Crider Antiques.

## Come a little closer
Scarf pins positioned in the ancient game of hunter and the hunted. Fly scarf pin of 14k. gold with an especially fine sapphire, four diamonds and a ruby, American, circa 1880, $800-1000. / Fly scar pin of gold with a turquoise body, six pearls, a ruby and two emeralds, circa 1865, $650-850. / Spider scarf with three rubies and a twenty-point diamond, American, circa 1880, $700-900. Private collection through Leonard D. Prins.

**A race to the rosebud**
Butterfly brooch of gold with shaped rock crystal plaques covering iridescent real butterfly wings, the body set with old-cut diamonds and ruby eyes, engraved Gebrauchs Musterschultz, circa 1900, $1500-2000. / Mid-Victorian spray brooch of gold and silver with rosebud mounted *en tremblant* and butterfly set with diamonds and rubies, $2500-3200. / Edwardian butterfly set with ruby antennae and opal and diamond wings mounted *en tremblant*, $3500-4000. Phillips Auction.

**Not the Skater's Waltz**
A crowd has gathered for playful fun. Airplane pendant of platinum and diamond, circa 1930, $450-600. / Victorian diamond and gold sunburst pendant/brooch circa 1865, $6500-7500. / Butterfly pendant of gold and plique-à-jour enamel, circa 1900, $2000-2500. / Bird of platinum with star sapphire and diamond, $800-1200. N. Bloom & Son.

**A gossamer butterfly**
Victorian butterfly brooch in patriotic colors of opal, sapphire, ruby and diamond, $24,000-28,000. N. Bloom & Son.

**Off for a paddleboat ride**
Flying geese brooch of platinum and diamonds, circa 1930s, $2650-3000. / Victorian diamond tremblant butterfly brooch, circa 1870, $6000-7500. / Victorian rose diamond duck stick pin, circa 1860, $750-900. / Diamond sea horse and Jimminy Cricket brooch, 1930s, $1800-2250. / Butterfly brooch of jade, opal and tourmaline, circa 1880, $2500-2650. N. Bloom & Son.

**A grand illusion**
Delicate butterfly brooch with four matching opals set as wings with diamonds surrounding, and a body of two pink sapphires with eyes of ruby cabochons, circa 1880, $24,000-28,000. Bentley & Co. Ltd.

## Little tremblers to amuse you

If you look closely, you will see little flyers on each of these brooches with trembling parts. A swarm of golden fireflies by Marcel Boucher, $450-600. / Brooch and earrings of multicolored blowers, $150-200. / Gold and rhinestone bee, $135-175. / Red mushroom and bee, $95-135. / Golden flower with bee inside by Hattie Carnegie, $175-250. / Rhinestone flower and hummingbird, $195-245. / Green grasshopper, $70-95. / Yellow enameled flowers and bee, $65-85. / Plant with butterfly and ladybug, $75-125. / Golden apple, $60-75. Norman Crider Antiques.

## From Russia with love

Butterfly brooch of Russian plique-à-jour enamel with diamond, sapphire, and pearl, and edged with small synthetic calibré rubies, $4000-5000. Christie's London.

**Good disguise**
Can you find the ten translucent plastic brooches hiding in this
field of flowers? E. & J. Antiques. $95-200 each.

**I see it clearly now**
Sterling silver and clear Lucite form the insect brooches gathered around a pair of similar earrings. Earrings and all-clear fly and spider by Trifari; $175-225, $300-400, and $350-450, respectively. Two spiders with rhinestones set in Lucite by Coro, $350-550 each. Moth with metal wings unmarked, $250-375. Joan Rothstein Tobobrowsky of E. & J. Rothstein Antiques.

**They gather together**
The pink plastic flower brooch attracts a swarm (clockwise from bottom to left): a pearl and rhinestone bug brooch by Nettie Rosenstein, $175-225. / A green enamel bug brooch by Trifari, $135-195. / A bug brooch with purple and pink glass stones by Trifari, $175-250. / An unmarked dragonfly brooch, $100-150. / A marvelous big bird brooch by Marcel Bocher, $500-750. / And a frog brooch by Trifari, $175-250. The flower itself is appraised at $100-125. Joan Rothstein Toborowsky of E. & J. Rothstein Antiques.

**The study collection is in place**

LEFT from top: Butterfly brooch of sapphire, rose diamond, emerald and cultured pearl, $550-850. / Dragonfly brooch of pink, blue and white glass stones, $95-125. / Black and white enamel ladybird brooch with diamond eyes and leaves and a branded onyx body, $500-700. / Bar brooch with fly of half-pearl, coral and gems, $175-225. / Bar brooch with cabochon garnet and applied rose diamond fly motif, $175-275. / Bar brooch with fly of rose diamond, ruby and pearl, $250-350. / Butterfly brooch of sapphire, rose diamond, ruby, half pearl and demantoid garnet. / CENTER, from top: Butterfly pendant of gold with diamond, ruby and sapphire, $500-650. / Butterfly brooch of ruby, emerald and diamond, $550-750. / Crescent brooch with butterfly of sapphire and half pearl, $350-425. / Butterfly brooch of 9k. gold, amethyst and half-pearl, $175-250. / Gold engraved butterfly brooch, $175-250. / Butterfly brooch of opal, sapphire and half-pearl, $250-425. / Fly stick pin of rose diamond, sapphire and pearl, $800-1000. / Tiny bee brooch of rose diamond, half-pearl and gem, $145-200. / Butterfly brooch of ruby, sapphire, rose diamond and half-pearl with detachable fittings, $1200-1400. / RIGHT, from top: Butterfly brooch of garnets, $250-400. / Fly stick pin of engraved gold, $175-250. / Bar brooch with butterfly of sapphire, rose diamond and half pearl, $275-375. / Bar brooch with dragonfly of turquoise and half-pearl, $275-375. / Bar brooch with fly of sapphire, half-pearl and pearl, $250-350. / Bar brooch with dragonfly of sapphire and half-pearl, $200-275. / Butterfly pendant or rose diamond, sapphire, ruby and half-pearl with detachable fitting, $850-1250. Christie's London.

**Swat!**
These critters know which side of the wall to stay on. Costume jewelry brooches of insects, none marked, circa 1960s. Beebe Hopper. $35-195 each.

**By the tranquil lake**
Dandelion brooch of 14k. gold with white and fancy natural yellow diamond, circa 1940, $5000-7500. / Edwardian style butterfly brooch of 18k. gold, sapphire and diamonds, $6800-8000. / Victorian butterfly brooch of opal, sapphire, ruby and diamonds, circa 1875, $10,000-13,000. / Butterfly brooch with flexible tail, 14k. gold with ruby, sapphire and diamonds, circa 1940, $11,000-13,500. N. Bloom & Son.

**Oriental habitat**
Animals dominate this group from the 1960s, most designed by Hattie Carnegie: sitting Buddha $145-195, blue bangle $300-400, red bangle $325-450, light green elephant $200-275, and mythical animal brooch $200-275. The dark green elephant brooch with rider's pavilion is by Ken Lane, $200-275, and the black Indian elephant head pendant is by Nettie Rosenstein, $300-400. Cobra & Bellamy.

# *Beasts*

### Elephant business
Large elephant brooch mounted with a large irregular-shaped baroque pearl and 18k. gold set with diamond toes, diamond eye, and mother-of-pearl tusks, $875-1100. Small elephant brooch with the body mounted with a dark grey baroque pearl and diamond pavé-set legs, head, and ruby eye, $1000-1250. Phillips Auction.

### Plastic fancies
Two unsigned plastic designs from the 1940s; a black glove with a bright red heart on a chain, "My heart is in my hand," $225-350; and an impish yellow elephant with a leather ear, $145-200. Bill and Dee Battle.

### The ear is clear
Lucite forms the ears of these unmarked plastic brooches from the 1950s. The white elephant's ears are pinned to swing freely, $175-225, while the thin Lucite pachyderm has his fixed and straight out, $125-185. Their green rabbit friend twists his ears in all directions, $100-150. Only their white celluloid pet dog with the red collar ribbon has his ears to the ground, $95-135.
Norman Crider.

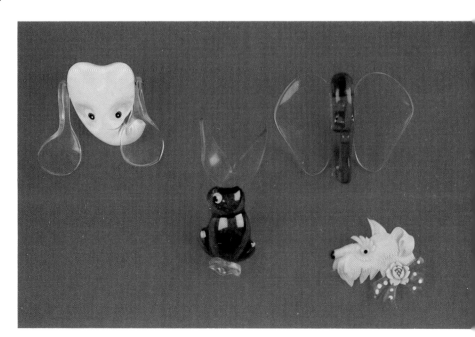

## Jelly bellies
Clear Lucite was molded as the dominant feature of this group of brooches, circa 1945, with sterling and gold washed details. Many of these forms were made by Trifari, here including the large pig, horse head, poodle dog and rabbit. The others are equally interesting but unmarked. Joan Rothstein Toborowsky of E. & J. Rothstein. $200-750 each.

## Not to be out-foxed
Only the clever-minded would design so dynamic a brooch as this, pavé-set with diamond and ruby cabochon eyes. Philips Auction. $900-1100.

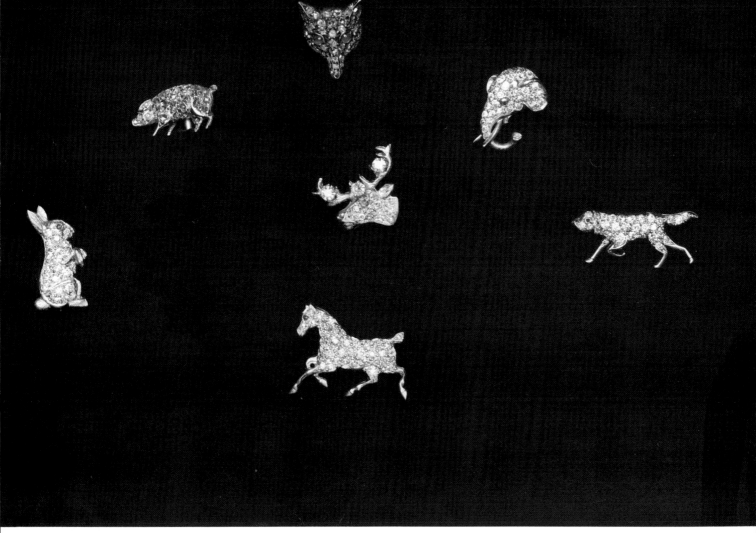

## Lively scarf pins

From the top: Fox pin of 14k. gold with 37 rose diamonds and ruby eyes, French, circa 1870, $900-1100. / Elephant head pin of platinum and 14k. gold with 36 diamonds and a ruby eye, by J.E. Caldwell & Co., $900-1100. / Pointing dog pin of platinum and 14k. gold, 32 diamonds and a ruby eye, by Tiffany & Co., $850-1000. / Trotting horse pin of platinum and 14k. gold with 36 diamonds and a ruby eye, $900-1100. / Sitting rabbit pin of platinum with 19 diamonds and a ruby eye, $900-1100. / Antique pig pin with 26 rose diamonds, circa 1890, $900-1100. / Elk head pin platinum and 14k gold with 15 diamonds and a sapphire, made in U.S.A., $1000-1200. Private collection through Leonard D. Prins.

## Cunning Teddy
Gold bear cub brooch with gem-set eye and nose. N. Bloom & Son. $1250-1500.

### Riches of the Orient
Grey pearls and matching spacers elegantly connect coral colored plastic faces with the matching elephant pendant, designed by Hattie Carnegie, circa 1965. Lucia Lambert. $800-1050.

### Luscious Lucite
Fine horse head and prancing gazelle brooches of Lucite with sterling, circa 1940, unmarked, $375-500 and $300-400 respectively. / Very unusual squirrel brooch of enameled sterling with Lucite tail by Corocraft, circa 1944, $350-500. / Wonderful pig brooch of Lucite, rhinestones and sterling by Trifari, circa 1944. $350-475. Clive Kandel.

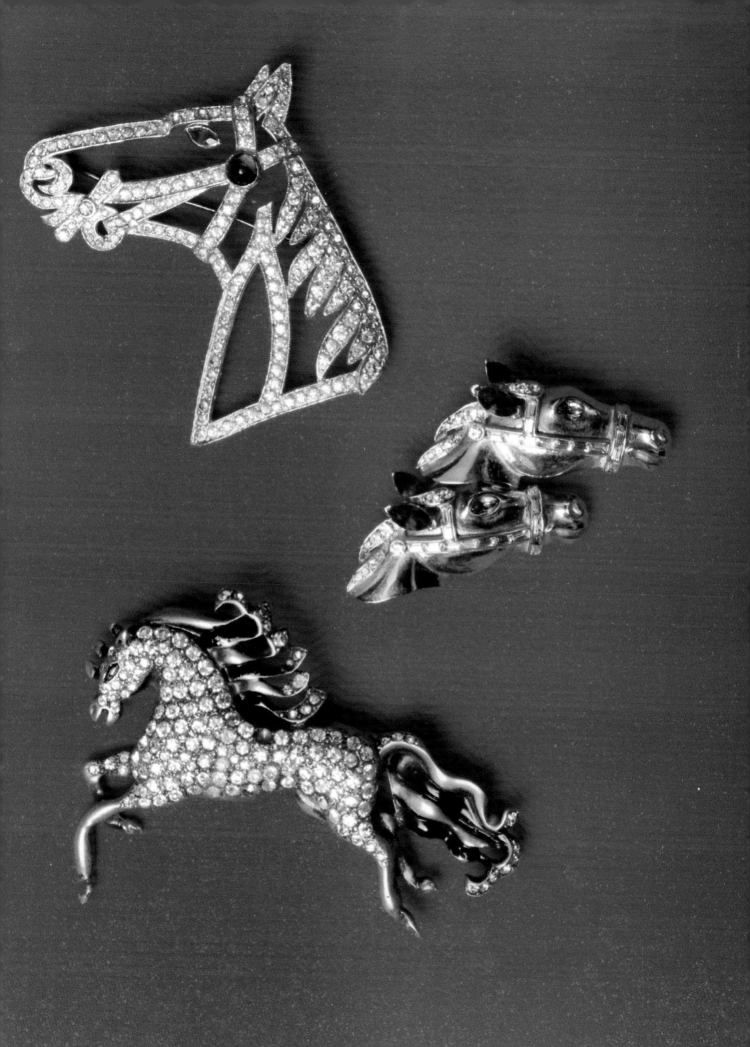

**Horsehead duets**
Duet brooches and clips can be worn separately or on an ingenious frame together. These horsehead duet brooches are part of a costume jewelry line by Coro called Duette, one pair with matching earrings. Norman Crider Antiques. Duettes, $200-375 each; earrings, $75-125/pair.

*Opposite page:*
*Top:* **Equestrian elegance**
Horsehead brooch of 9k. gold with ruby eye, $700-850. / Two mare and foal brooches of 9k. textured gold, $650-800 each. / Victorian horseshoe brooch, $200-275. N. Bloom & Son.

*Bottom:* **Be my valentine**
A little plush bear brooch with a big message spelled out on red plastic. Norman Crider Antiques. $95-145.

## Monkey business
Playful monkeys captured in amusing poses by costume jewelry designers, these unmarked. Norman Crider Antiques. $75-275 each.

## Wild rascals
A sterling brooch depicting a bear cub in a unicycle with a spinning wheel, $95-145. / Panda bear brooch pavé-set with clear and black rhinestones and a red eye, $100-150. / Animated lion brooch of gold washed metal rhinestones, $65-95. / Textured walrus brooch by Erwin Pearl, $100-150. / Startled tiger with enameled details, unmarked, $100-150. Norman Crider Antiques.

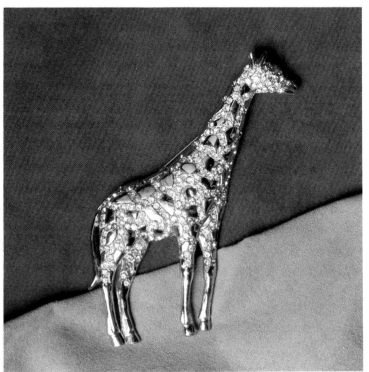

**Precious plastic**
Experiments with plastic in the 1940s produced a wide array of delightful jewelry types, as these pins exemplify. The double horse designs are French, others unmarked. Cobra and Bellamy. $125-325 each.

**Head above it all**
Spectacular giraffe brooch by Coro set with clear rhinestones and a red eye, circa 1938. Clive Kandel. $300-400.

**Canine friends**
Victorian 15k. gold Highland terrier brooch with diamond eyes circa 1875, $750-1000. / Pair of greyhounds in a brooch of gold with ruby and diamond collars, $2750-3500. / Retriever brooch of 9k. gold, $500-600. N. Bloom & Son.

**Valliant stallions**
In the 1940s, the movies popularized romantic, heroic figures who rode wild horses, defended the oppressed and languished in tropical paradise. These plastic molded brooches, and many other designed along the same themes, carried the movie images to the everyday man. Bess Goodson. $150-350 each.

**House pets**
Stylish dogs are popular costume jewelry designs. Jumping Poodle brooch with blue glass eye by Joseff of Hollywood, circa 1945, $195-275. / Dachshund on the stairs brooch by Kramer of New York, early 1950s, $250-350. / Sweet-faced spaniel brooch, unmarked, $175-250. Norman Crider Antiques.

**Buttons and pins**
Plastics were molded into an endless variety of accessory items in the 1940s. Here are four elephant buttons of red plastic, $65-85; / a clear molded Scotty dog pin, $65-95; / the Cow Jumping Over the Moon in molded celluloid, $75-100; / Wise Old Owl in green and brown mottled and carved plastic, $100-150; / a mottled green Scotty dog, $70-90; / and a mischievous wooden carved cat with a Lucite fish bowl mounted as a brooch, $225-275. Bess Goodson.

**The menagerie**
A collection of animal costume jewelry lovingly assembled and chosen for their charming designs, 1950s and 1960s. Beebe Hopper. $25-75 each.

## Delightful duets

Coro Duettes are imaginative and whimsical as these examples demonstrate so charmingly. The crowns with green glass stones are joined by matching earrings, $400-500/set. / Two monkeys perch and amuse us with their grimace, $350-400. / The rabbit faces are alive with animation, $350-400. / Acorns and oak leaves also have matching earrings, early 1960s, $450-550/set. Norman Crider Antiques.

### Wabbits!

A posh gentleman rabbit brooch with top hat and crane, unmarked, $70-90. / Rabbits out of a hat in a three piece set of brooch and earrings in sterling silver, $175-225/set. / Hungry little rabbit brooch by Marcel Boucher, 1950s, $145-195. / Rabbit with the blue ears clip, late 1940s, $125-175. Norman Crider Antiques.

# People

**Tremblers from around the world**
In costumes of diverse civilizations, these unmarked brooches mounted *en tremblant* from the 1940s display people in their different lifestyles. Norman Crider Antiques. $175-375 each.

*Opposite page:*
**Genie with a crystal ball**
The detail of this set should be carefully examined. Each piece has a different Genie. The earrings, necklace, bracelet and three brooches were made by HAR, circa 1955. May all your wishes come true. Clive Kandel. $1500-2000/all.

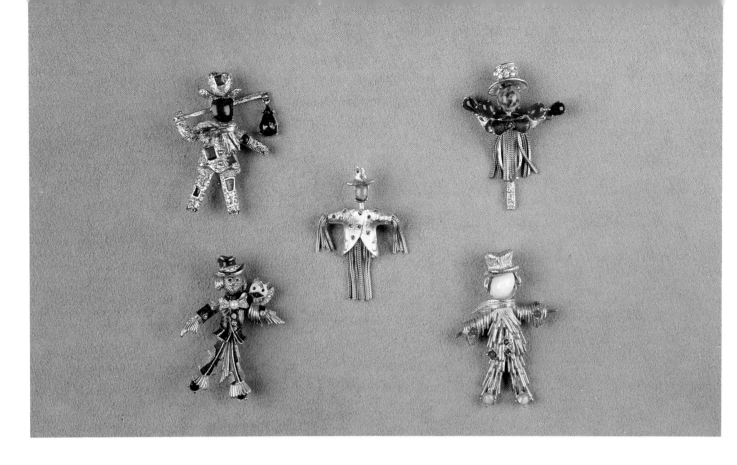

**Scarecrows**
A hobo brooch by Florenza surveys a field with four scarecrow brooches. Only the one with the pink face is signed by Pauline Rader, circa 1960. Norman Crider Antiques. Hobo $145-185, scarecrows $150-225 each.

**Walking the dog**
Variations on a theme in costume jewelry. Only the pair at the far right, the dog walking the dog, is signed Starter. Norman Crider Antiques. $125-225 each.

**Meant to amuse**
The lively designs of these clear plastic brooches are highlighted by tinted details, a method found to be effective in this modern jewelry material. E. & J. Rothstein Antiques. $250-450 each.

**All set to delight and amuse**
Boy and girl clips of 18k. gold set with moonstone, emerald, diamond and ruby, circa 1950, $1800-2000. / Jester brooch of 18k. red and yellow gold set with gems, circa 1950, $1750-2000. N. Bloom & Son.

**Clowning around again**
The costumes of this group of clown brooches are meant only to amuse and relax the crowd. They bring a smile every time. Norman Crider Antiques. $100-300 each.

*Opposite page:*
**Blackamoors**
Exotic African figures were romanticized in theaters in the 1960s. Blackamoor brooch in jeweled cap with pearl drops by Nettie Rosenstein, circa 1965, $650-950. / Blackamoor brooch with a red stone in his turban by Ciner, circa 1965, $650-850. / Blackamoor brooch with jeweled bodice by Ciner, circa 1965, $700-900. / Enameled gold Blackamoor clip copied from a design by Cartier, Paris, 1938, no value available. Clive Kandel.

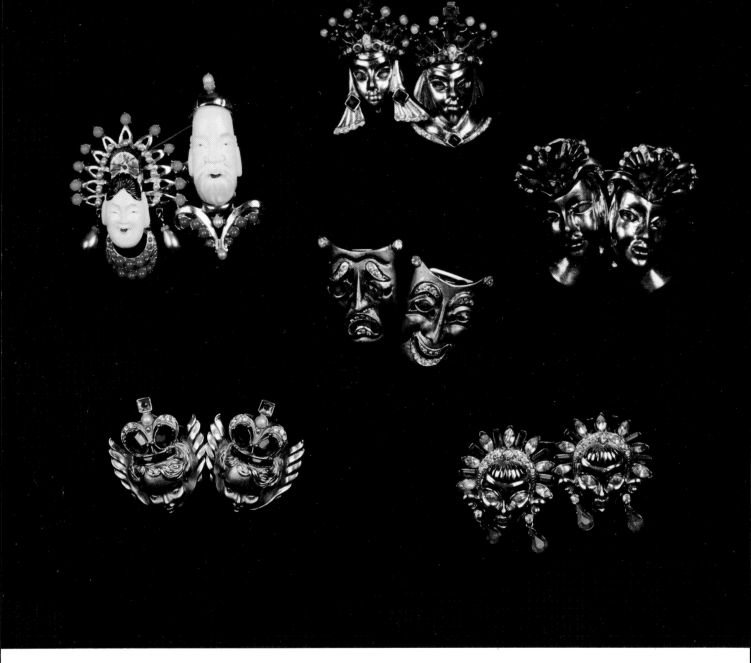

**At the masked ball**
Six pairs of Coro Duette brooches depicting different mask designs,
circa 1950. Norman Crider Antiques. $400-800 each.

*Opposite page:*
**Chinese ivory**
A perky Chinese boy's face, made to resemble ivory, appears on
each of these by HAR, circa 1955. There are four bracelets, a chain
necklace with pendant, brooch and earrings in the set. Clive Kandel.
$1500-2000/all.

**Tropical dancer**
This sterling silver set of brooch and earrings were made by Corocraft circa 1945. Today, collectors may want to call it Josephine Baker. Clive Kandel. $800-1000/set.

**The Medusa head and the merman**
Inspired by a Renaissance jewel with Baroque pearl in the treasury of the Grand Duke of Tuscany in Florence, this brooch of enamel and faux pearls was created by Hattie Carnegie, circa 1974, $750-950. Clive Kandel.

**Memories of Thailand**
Silver and faux coral are wrought and carved to create this matching set of jewelry of Oriental inspiration. Unmarked, circa 1955. Clive Kandel. $600-800/set.

**Born to dance**
The ballroom dancers brooches (one large and two small) and earrings (small) are by Mosell, $200-350 each. / Siamese dancer with blue and green stones by Marcel Boucher, circa 1950, $175-225. / Golden Siamese dancer, unmarked, $100-150. / Japanese dancer by Nettie Rosenstein, $200-300. / Black Siamese dancer marked Sterling, $225-325. / Spanish dancers, unmarked, $95-175 each. Norman Crider Antiques.

**Musicians take note**
Everybody can play; you just have to find the right instruments. Each of these figures is a brooch, and the banjo player can sway to the rhythm because his arms and legs are hinged. Norman Crider Antiques. Small brooches, $95-145 each; tall banjo player, $200-275.

## That's entertainment
Minstrels in blackface are recalled by these brooches, unmarked except for the binoculars and the watermelon by BSK, each $100-150. Small minstrel face $75-125, large minstrel face $150-200, blackamoor figure $145-195, and minstrel with hat $175-225. Norman Crider Antiques.

## Going to a show
The animated dancer brooch, by Corocraft circa 1950, seems to beckon to the superbly designed two sailors brooch by Marcel Boucher, circa 1942. Clive Kandel. Dancer $165-225, sailors $350-550.

## They wore their patriotism for all to see

Pride in American success during World War II was exhibited by wearing this jewelry. Sterling B-52 airplane brooch, $2000-2500. / Jeweled airplane brooch by Trifari, $225-275. / Enameled V for victory brooch with flyer's wings, $100-150. / Red plastic buckle with enameled metal V and skating star Sonya Heyne's image, $175-275. / Small blue enameled brooch with "Victory" and pendant Marine Corps insignia, $75-125. / Large jeweled propeller and wings brooch, $175-245. Norman Crider Antiques.

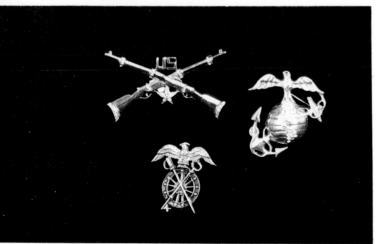

## For use on any costume

Civilians in the 1940s were proud to wear these costume jewelry interpretations of insignia from the U.S. Army Infantry, $125-175; Marine Corps, $100-150; and Army Quartermaster Corps, $125-175. Norman Crider Antiques.

**Carry a touch for Liberty**
The patriotic theme of the 1940s was carried high in costume jewelry, especially with this interpretation of the Statue of Liberty's torch by Staret. Norman Crider Antiques. $650-850.

**Anchors away**
Brooch designed as an anchor with chain, circa 1925. Phillips Auction. $4500-5500.

**Remember the troops**
Soldiers were honored by these brooch designs, including the band members who stirred up the patriotism. Brass sailor figure with enamel, $75-100. / Three wooden cut-outs with painted details and movable plastic eyes, $95-175. / Cast lead drum major and drummer with enamel decoration, $125-175 each. Norman Crider Antiques.

**Ethnic costumes**
Cultural interest in foreign people is noted by these clips which represent Tyrolean, Dutch, Chinese, and Japanese figures. Only the red and white clip is signed, by Marcel Boucher, circa 1945. Norman Crider Antiques. $200-400 each.

**Cossack dancers**
Lively steps are implied by these brooches from the 1950s. The man in by Trifari. The lady is unmarked. Norman Crider Antiques. $150-225 each.

**Sing and dance**
An enameled metal minstrel figure with diamond-studded concertina taps out a song on a base of pyrite. Christie's, London.

**Fancy frills**
Hobé & Cie created these lavish pieces circa 1945. The all rhinestone figure belts out a ballad, $150-200. / Pendant and matching earrings feature a molded portrait of a woman surrounded with fine metalwork and rhinestones, $400-500/set. Golden mesh bracelet shows chain and tassel details, $300-400. Beebe Hopper.

**Westward-ho!**
Plastics and brass are cast into light-hearted brooches depicting the people and animals of the wild west. Norman Crider Antiques. $100-350 each.

**Clearly collectible**
These clear Lucite brooches from the
1940s entice a collector to find other
designs in this range. Good luck! E. & J.
Rothstein. $175-400 each.

*Opposite page:*
*Top:* **In the Age of Chivalry**
Knight's helmet brooch of gold and silver, red guilloché enamel and diamonds,
circa 1900. $2250-2500/ Violin brooch pavé-set with diamonds. $2750-3500. N.
Bloom & Son.

*Bottom:* **Celebrate with music**
Green plastic brooch formed as a violin and bow and marked An Airfix Product.
Made in England, circa 1945. Cobra & Bellamy, London. $350-500.

In Exercise 88 you'll be using a new fingering on some of the G's. In measure 4 and 7 the G is preceded by B♭. You shouldn't slide your third finger over to the first string so play the G with the fourth finger.

THE GOLDEN VANITY

**Strum me a tune**
Clear and black plastic banjo brooches from the 1940s.
E. & J. Rothstein. $175-250 each.

**Anyone for a round of golf?**
This caddy knows the greens. The other players must have some pretty fancy shots, judging from their bags. None marked. Norman Crider Antiques. Caddy $300-400, large bag $75-100, small bag $50-95.

**Comic characters**
Charlie McCarthy is portrayed in a clip with a mouth that opens, $200-300. / Li'l Abner is shown in a brooch with his characteristic running pose, circa 1955, $225-275. Norman Crider Antiques.

**A painter's palette**
Copper brooch and earrings designed as the tools of an artist.
Jackie Fleischman. $145-195/set.

**Sea goddess**
Marvelous clear plastic face brooch with golden metal and rhine-stones by Fred A. Block, circa 1942, $800-1200. / Fish clip with great style of clear plastic and rhinestones by Trifari, circa 1941, $400-500. Clive Kandel.

**Flowers for sale**
A picturesque French street vendor of flowers is portrayed in this brooch of gold wires and gemstones, circa 1940. N. Bloom & Son. $8000-9000.

**A touch of Lucite**
Artists have experimented with plastics since the 1920s and these are
some of their efforts. Only the necklace pendant is marked FNCo. Joan
Rothstein Toborowsky of E. & J. Rothstein Antiques. $300-1000 each.

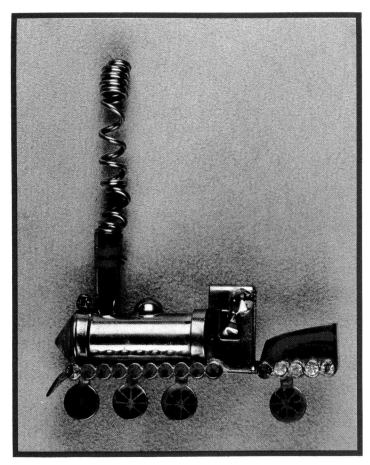

**Illusion insured**
Mask brooch of enameled copper, circa 1950s. $175-235.
Bizarre Bazaar.

**Steaming right along**
Amusing metal train brooch with stencil decorated wheels and
sporting colored rhinestone accents. Norman Crider Antiques.
$165-225.

**Little red schoolhouse**
Molded plastic forms the designs of the
schoolhouse with a door hinged to open
when the ball is pulled. Norman Crider
Antiques. $175-245.

*Opposite page:*
**Time for champagne**
Let the corks fly when you wear this jewelry. Champagne glass
brooch with iridescent and clear stones by B. David, circa 1960,
$135-185. / Pearl bubbles top this champagne glass brooch by Pell,
circa 1955, $165-225. / Pearl bracelet with champagne bucket
pendant, circa 1960, $60-80. / Sterling silver musical note and
champagne glass pendant with pearl bubbles, circa 1958, $200-
250. / Bracelet of golden chain and champagne glass pendant with
pearl bubbles, circa 1958, $100-150. Clive Kandel.

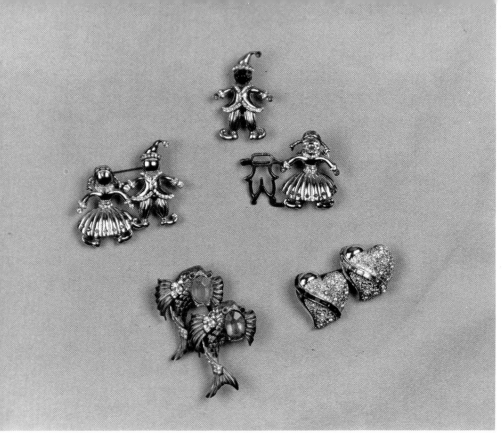

**A couple of couples**
Two Coro Duette brooches which are mirror images in design, have different coupling frames, and are variously set with rhinestones, 1950s. Norman Crider Antiques. Couple duettes $150-225 each; fish duette $200-250; heart duette $125-175.

**Dance the Bacchanal**
Coro Duette clip depicting ballerina Anna Pavlova as a Bacchanal dancer, circa 1950. Norman Crider Antiques. $600-850.

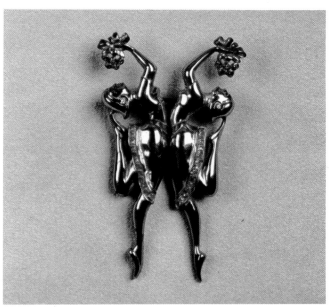

**Chessmen**
The King, Queen and Horse figures from a chess set are depicted as clips by Trifari, circa 1945. Clive Kandel. $150-225 each.

*Opposite page:*
**Ornaments for the Christmas season**
Santa with his friends and traditional ornaments depicted as unmarked earrings and brooches from the 1970s. Beebe Hopper. $25-100 each.

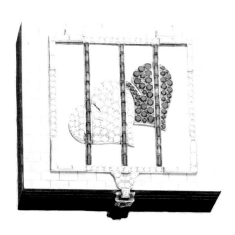

## Imprisoned love

18k. three color gold powder compact with lid designed as prison walls and two trapped hearts set with diamonds, rubies, and calibré sapphires. The clasp is designed as a diamond padlock. Made by Henry Elisha, England. Phillips Auction. $5000-6800.

## A cherubs duet

Golden cherubs transport a clear heart and star marked DEC in this duet brooch by Coro Duette, circa 1955. Norman Crider Antiques. $395-550.

## A bleeding heart

Antique Jaipur enamel heart-shaped pendant set with diamonds, bird design on the reverse. Bonham's Auction.

## For a heart to heart conversation

This spectacular necklace would surely provoke serious discussion between the giver and the recipient. Baroque-cultured pearls separated by bold rondels support a double heart pendant of carved emerald and carved ruby surrounded by diamonds. Christie's, New York. $8000-10,000.

*Opposite page:*
## Cherubs hard at work

The gallant knight on this sweater pin by Coro, attached by chains to his sword-pierced heart, is an easy mark for the cherubs; knight $500-750. / Cupid as a rhinestone and golden brooch carries time as a pendant watch marked Balta, $625-725. / A Coro Duette brooch and matching earrings of cherubs carrying a green rhinestone heart and a star marked AUG, circa 1955, $500-700/set. Clive Kandel.

**The gift of a Valentine**
Jeweled heart motifs proclaim enduring love. Cupid and a large red stone are mounted above two blue hearts on this unmarked brooch circa 1939, $400-500. / Blue hearts dominate these earrings and matching crowned brooch of sterling silver by Corocraft, circa 1945, $500-650/set. / Blue enamel and rhinestones form a bow brooch and pendant heart by Coro, circa 1938, $225-275. / A rhinestone arrow pierces two blue hearts in a brooch by Trifari, circa 1943, $185-225. / The red heart with comet tail was created by Mimi diN, circa 1965, $275-375. Clive Kandel.

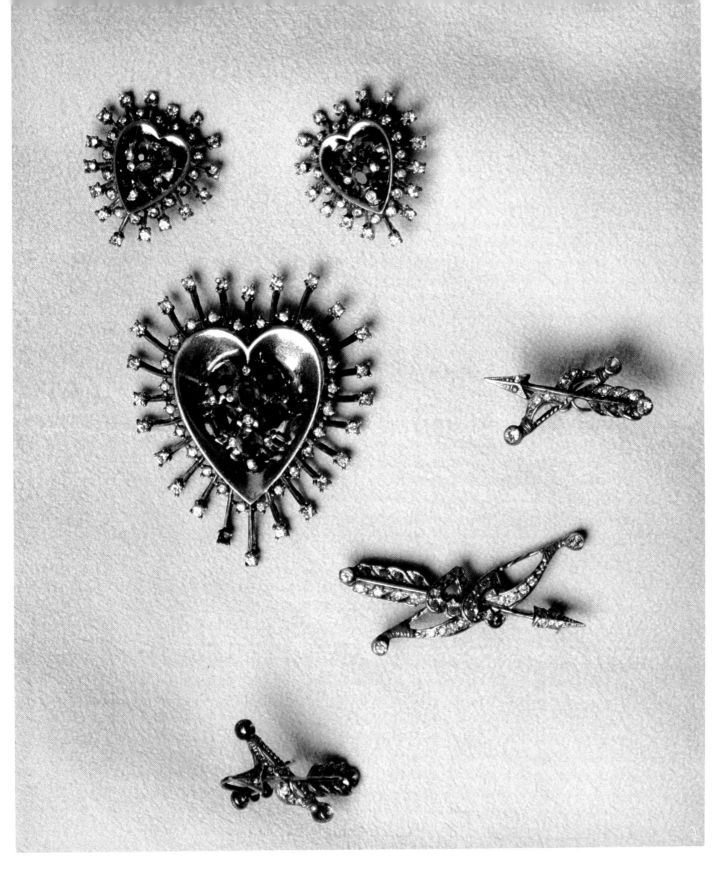

**Symbols of romance**
Heart-shaped clip and earrings by Trifari with radiating rhinestone frames, $350-500/set. Cupid's bow and arrow set with rhinestones and enamel accents in an unmarked brooch and earrings, circa 1944, $200-275/set. Clive Kandel.

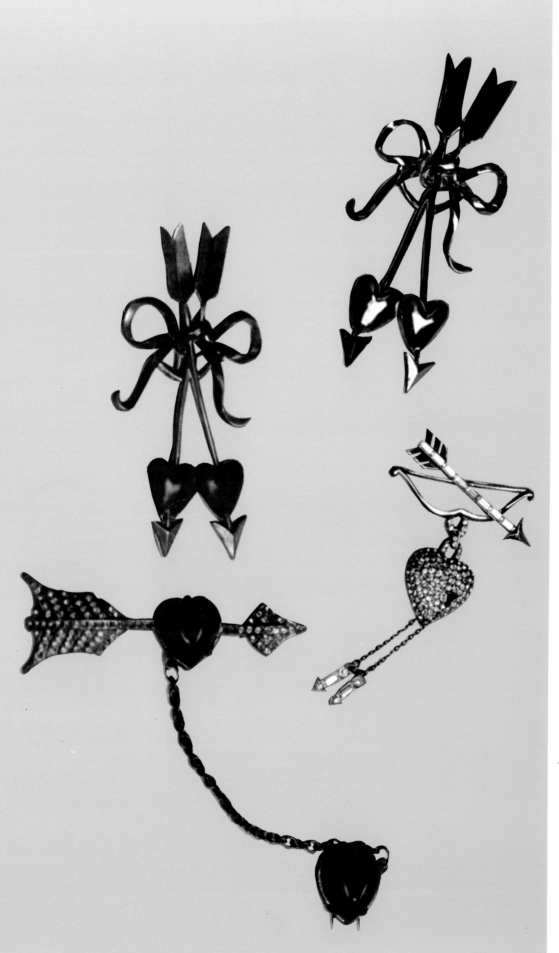

**Captured hearts**
Pierced hearts are the fruits of Cupid's adventures. Golden bow knot and arrow brooch marked Coro, $200-250, and an identical design in pot metal with blue and red painted decoration without markings, $135-185, both circa 1938. / Bow and arrow brooch with an unusual heart pendant pierced by two arrows on a connecting chain, marked Sterling, circa 1942. $200-250/ Rhinestone arrow brooch with a golden chain joining a red clip, circa 1938. $185-250.. Clive Kandel.

*Opposite page:*
*Bottom left:* **Art Nouveau remembrance**
Heart-shaped locket of 14k. gold with a scrolled relief design, circa 1900. Sandy DeMaio. $275-350.

*Top right:* **They say it was Witchcraft**
Brooches to enhance the romantic atmosphere. Man in the moon by P.E.P. $125-175/ Heart and hands clip unmarked. $245-295/ Golden bat clip unmarked. $120-145/ Devil by ...SRRIA ARGENTIN. $100-150. Norman Crider Antiques.

*Bottom right:* **The results of imagination**
A cupid brooch of gold set with gem stones by Van Cleef and Arpels, 1940s. $800-900/ Safe Cracker lapel watch of gold where the safe door opens to reveal a watch face, 1960s. $1250-1500. N. Bloom & Son.

**A starlet is born**
Sterling silver cuff bracelet with an oval medallion bearing the relief image of a young woman and three pierced stars by Joseff of Hollywood, circa 1945. Muriel Karasik. $500-750.

**Sweetness in miniature**
A tiny painting of two Dutch girls on the back of a crystal is mounted in front of a real butterfly wing in this pendant. N. Bloom & Son. $400-600.

**Clear cupidity**
Bracelet with a crystal panel bound by a cast silver link band which includes four figures of cupid. Jackie Fleischman. $195-245.

**Dance the cachucha**
Silver buckle and pendant of openwork panels with Spanish style dancer and faceted red stones in the frames Jackie Fleischman. $200-285/set.

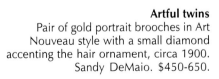

**Artful twins**
Pair of gold portrait brooches in Art Nouveau style with a small diamond accenting the hair ornament, circa 1900. Sandy DeMaio. $450-650.

### Micro-mosaic magic
Apollo and a pair of cupids conveyed the love of the original giver to the original receiver of this magnificent pendant and earring set composed of micro-mosaic stones in gold and enameled frames, Italian in the Renaissance revival style of the mid-19th century. Sandy DeMaio. $2000-3000/set.

### Fine Italian goldwork
The careful manipulation of gold is expertly displayed in the interesting frame with fringe dangles which surrounds a hardstone cameo of a woman in this brooch, Italian circa 1870. John Joseph. $3200-3750.

**A mighty triumvirate**
Three fine cameos, two of hardstones (of a woman and a bearded man) and one of jasperware ceramic of a man with Georgian hair style, each set in a gold frame, English, 19th century. Diana Foley. Woman $2250-2750, bearded man $2750-3000, jasperware $2500-2750.

**The art of artifice**
An enameled gold brooch bearing the portrait of a woman decorated in Art Nouveau style, the contrived prevailing fashion at the turn of the century. Sandy DeMaio. $600-900.

**A cherished memento**
Hardstone cameo of a woman's head portrait set in an exquisite gold and enamel pendant frame of floral design with pearls, late 19th century. Diana Foley. $3500-4500.

**Sentimental portraiture**
Photographs of loved ones are mounted in these portrait pins and buttons from the early 20th century. E. & J. Rothstein Antiques. $85-145 each.

**And what is your song?**
A late 19th century French brooch of gold with enamel painting of a woman with a mandolinand small green gemstones set in her cap. Sandy DeMaio. $400-500.

**Victorian romanticism**
Carved coral cherub and goddess figures are mounted in garlands of leaves studded with diamond on this pendant from the mid-19th century. Bonham's Auction. $1500-1800.

**Coral transformed**
Mediterranean coral carved as a woman's romanticized head portrait mounted in a gold frame as a brooch, mid-19th century. Sandy DeMaio. $600-750.

*Opposite page:* **With religious deities in mind**
Neckalce of gold with three onyx cameos of mythological scenes mounted between pearl an onyx amphora-shaped drops, and matching earrings, by Carlo Giuliano, circa 1870, $12,000-15,000/ set. / Hardstone cameo of Apollo's profile framed with pearls and mounted as a pendant, late 19th century, $3500-4800. / Two bracelets of gold links and cabochons of the twelve stones mentioned in the Book of Revelations as the foundations and gates of the heavenly Jerusalem (jasper, sapphire, chalcedony, emerald, sardonyx, sard, chrysolite, beryl, topaz, chrysophrase, jacinth and amethyst) by Carlo and Arthur Giuliano, circa 1900, $4000-6000. Sotheby's London.

*Above:* **Picture perfect**
Molded plastic resembling tortoiseshell bears the portrait likeness of a young girl with early 19th century hairdressing. The portrait is surrounded by a double row of rhinestones, circa 1960, by Dodds. Beebe Hopper. $75-100.

**Super sealing stones**
These hardstone carvings of human faces were mounted in gold as document sealing stones of the early 19th century, English. Wartski. $1250-1750/each.

**Aurora unchained**
The Roman goddess of the dawn is racing forth with her steeds on this early 19th century hardstone cameo, set in a gold pendant by John Brogden of London, circa 1870. Wartski. No value available.

## Classic designs
Gold and Roman mosaic brooch depicting a maenad, circa 1870, $400-500. / Early 19th century agate cameo of Jupite Ammon mounted in an octagonal engraved gold frame and wrist band, circa 1850, $1250-1500. Sotheby's London.

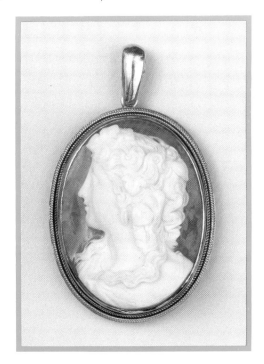

## A lady of the court
Hardstone cameo of a lady in 18th century court dress mounted in a French Brooch with diamonds in the frame. Bonham's Auction. $2500-3500.

## Cameo locket
An antique oval hardstone carved to depict a maiden's profile is mounted as a locket pendant with bead and wirework frame. Christie's London. $1500-1800.

## Minerva preserved
The Greek goddess of wisdom is carved in onyx and mounted in diamonds in this brooch, circa 1820. Wartski.

# High Flyers

**Patriotic emblems**
The American eagle theme was proudly worn in the 1940s when these brooches were made. The sterling silver eagle with gem-set arrows is by Corocraft. Norman Crider Antiques. $175-300 each.

*Opposite page:*
**"This weather is for the birds," she said.**
Antique jewelry is featured. Triple crescent pin of graduated diamonds set in platinum, late 19th century, $8000-9500. / Shooting star brooch of gold, moonstone, diamond and pearl, $1250-1550. / A golden flying goose brooch with enameled head, $600-850. / Silver hobo character brooch set with gemstones, $1750-2250. / Enameled bar pin labeled "Plus est en vous." $650-800. / Duck brooch of silver and gold, $375-500. / Grouse brooch of three colors of gold, $450-600. N. Bloom & Son.

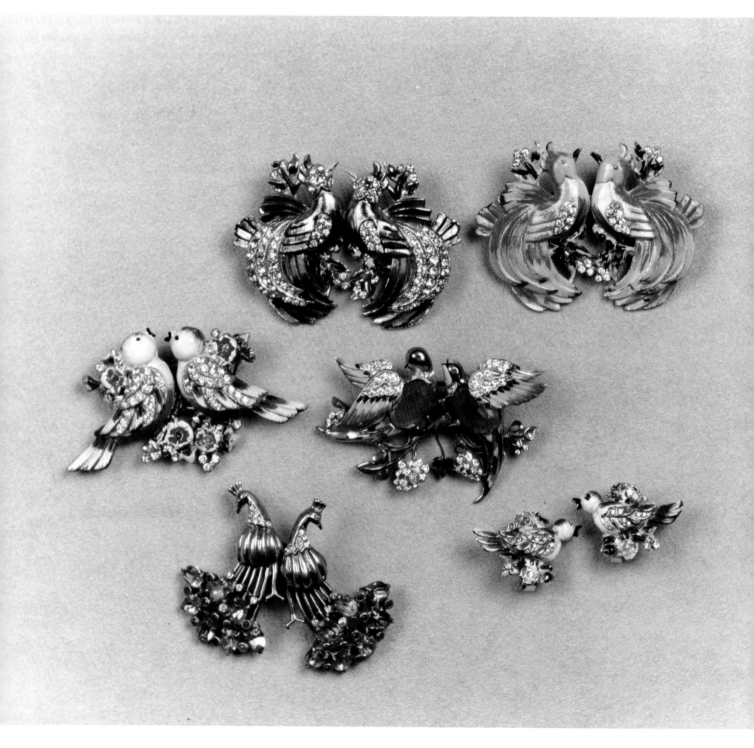

**A flock of duets**
Five duet pairs by Coro Duette and one pair of matching earrings. The peacocks and blue birds marked Sterling. Norman Crider Antiques. Top left $275-350, top right $300-375, middle left $350-500/set (with earrings at bottom right), middle right $325-375, bottom left $350-400.

**Duet bird set**
Matching necklace and duet pin in a double bird design by
Corocraft. Norman Crider Antiques. $650-850/set.

**Birds of a feather**
Wonderful group of matching duets comprising a
triple (the largest separated to show the ingenious
frame that joins the trio), a duet, and matching
earrings, all in sterling silver, Coro Duette by
Corocraft. Norman Crider Antiques. $750-1000/
group.

**Variations on a theme**
Six enamel and rhinestone decorated sterling duet brooches by Corocraft, three showing color and placement variations of birds from the same mold. Norman Crider Antiques. Top $300-350, center three $325-400 each, bottom left peacocks $475-650, bottom right $275-325.

### Birds on the move

Group of wonderfully imaginative trembling bird brooches in costume jewelry, all with moving parts. Two parrots on swings marked JJ. / Bird on nest with pearl eggs by Florenza, 1950s. / Red bird on gold branch by Castlecliff. / White enamel bird and leaves with blue accent by ART. / Yellow enameled duck by Marcel Boucher. / Three parakeets on branches by Staret. Other designs unmarked. Norman Crider Antiques. $75-200 each.

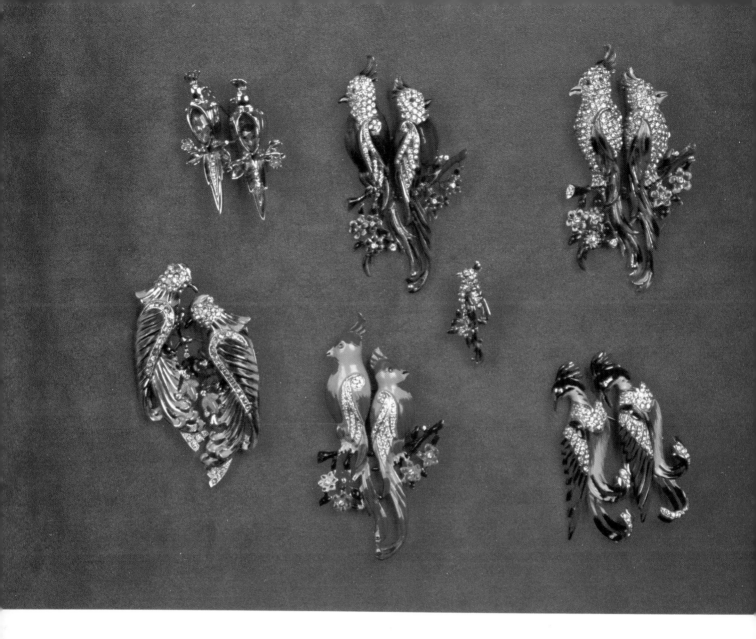

**Tropical pairs**
Six Coro Duette clips of slightly varying designs and
arrangements of stone settings, and one with matching
earrings. Norman Crider Antiques. $250-400.

**Quiet and patient**
Owl brooch of two-colored gold with diamond face and onyx eyes perched on a
branch. Phillips Action. $4500-6000.

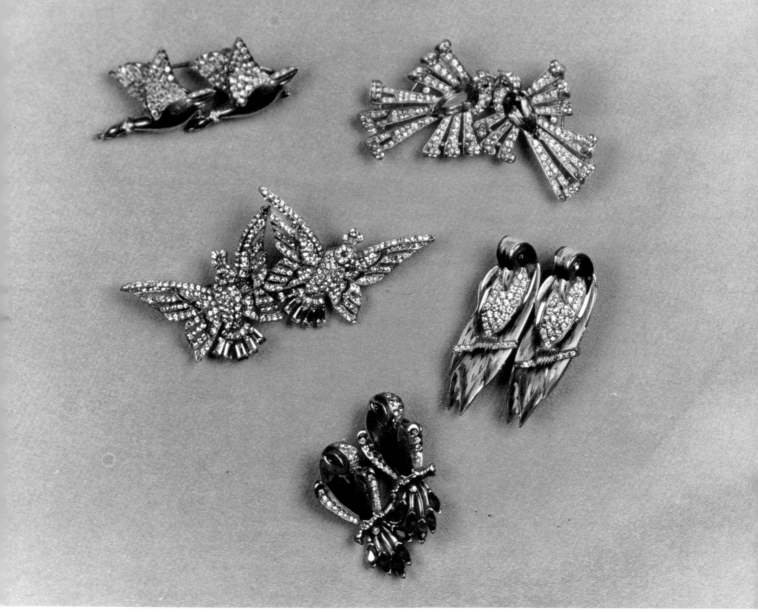

## Flying duets
Soaring geese duet brooch with rhinestone wings and green glass eyes, unmarked, $225-275. / Red and green bodies and rhinestones feathers on a pair of duet bird clips, Clip-Mates by Trifari, $250-300. / Delicate pavé openwork pair of Clip-Mates with red eyes by Trifari, $275-400. / Parrots of gold washed sterling silver and enamel by Coro Duette, $250-350. / Small pair of birds with gold washed sterling silver, green eyes and red tail feathers by Coro Duette, 1940s, $250-300. Norman Crider Antiques.

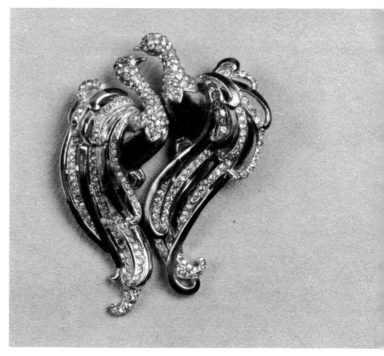

### Exotic giants
Enormous pair of Coro Duette bird clips, 3 1/2" long, with fluid feather design and interacting placement. Norman Crider Antiques. $800-1200.

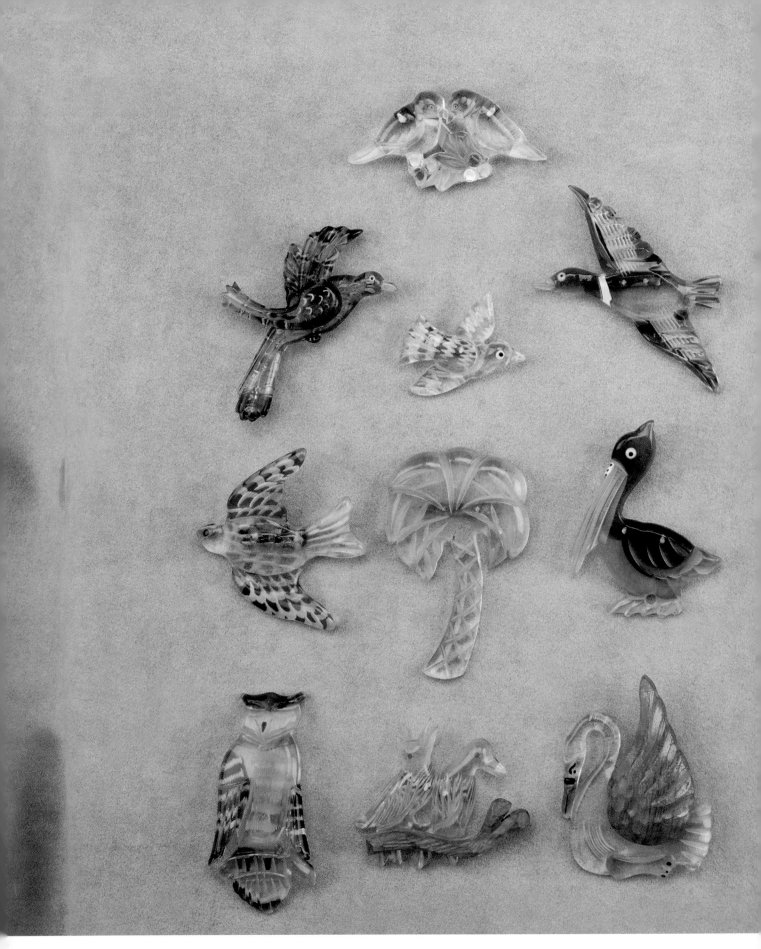

**Clearly wonderful**
Nineteen varieties of Lucite birds mingle with a palm three and an acorn in this array of brooches from the 1940s, none are marked by a maker. E. & J. Rothstein Antiques. $100-300 each.

**Portable aviaries**
Two brooches of costume jewelry designed as bow knots suspending
birds in cages, the one on the right marked Sterling, both circa 1945.
Clive Kandel. Left $195-245, right $250-325.

**Birdbath classics**
Sweater pin in two parts joined by a double chain, $395-495, and a matching solitary pin in a refreshing birdbath design of sterling silver and rhinestones by Coro, circa 1951, $325-425. Clive Kandel.

**Lucite favorites**
Clear Lucite molded as a bird and an umbrella with colored stain details, 1940s. Bill and Dee Battle. $125-175 each.

### Cute owls
Two sterling silver duet clips: a tripled graduated owl design with red stones, $375-450, and a dynamic yellow-eyed owl design with enamel in a clip with matching earrings, $400-500/set, both by Coro Duette. Norman Crider Antiques.

### Lovebirds
Coro Duette clips in lovebirds design which form a heart when joined. Norman Crider Antiques. $245-295.

**Collected wisdom**
Four Coro Duette clips in owl designs, one shown separated to demonstrate the connecting frame. Norman Crider Antiques. $225-325.

**Feathered friends**
Enameled owl and two parrots mounted as brooches by Trifari, circa 1969. Clive Kandel. Owl $115-165, parrots, $95-145 each.

**Whoo's minding the store while all these owls are gathered for the camera?**
Mother-of-Pearl, glass stones and cast base metals crate a delightful variety of costume designs, none marked. Beebe Hopper. $35-75 each.

**Hungry pelican**
Mechanical pelican designed circa 1940 by Marcel Bocher. The mouth features a rubber band mechanism which opens when the chain is pulled to reveal a fish. Brilliant! Clive Kandel. $500-750.

**To catch the coastal breeze**
Swedish two-color 18k. gold bird brooch with nephrite and coral mistletoe, 1952, $1850-2250. / Victorian navy pennant in enamel on gold, $950-1050. / Gold compass pendant, $500-650. / Bar brooch with two gem-set flies, $1000-1200. / Gold swallow brooch, $2800-3200. / Small invisibly-set gem tie tack in gold designed as an abstract hummingbird, $700-900. / Rose-diamond brooch depicting four birds on a branch, $1200-1400. / Victorian pavé-set diamond and demantoid garnet running fox brooch, $2250-2500. / Fox head brooch, $1000-1200. / 9k. gold retriever brooch, $450-600. / Gold brooch designed as a submarine, $450-600. N. Bloom & Son.

**Flying critters**
Birds give designers an unlimited opportunity to experiment with action forms, some streamlined and elegant others quite static and expressive. This group of unmarked costume jewelry brooches are from the 1950s and 1960s. Beebe Hopper. $35-85 each.

**Morning caller**
Rooster brooch with a freshwater baroque pearls and pavé diamonds, his comb and tail of calibré-cut rubies, sapphires and emeralds in silver and 18k. gold. Christie's New York. $2500-3250.

**Fish vs. fowl**
The enameled fish will be somebody's dinner. The hummingbird is by Staret, the fighting cock with orange legs is marked J., others not marked. Norman Crider Antiques. $85-175 each.

**Let her rip**
Paper knife of gold, the terminal set with a carved emerald owl with ruby eyes, the dart-shaped blade applied with a diamond-set flowerhead, Russian, circa 1900. Sotheby's London. $5000-7000.

**Ruffled feathers**
Startled owl clip/brooch with ruby cabochon eyes. Phillips Auction. $500-650.

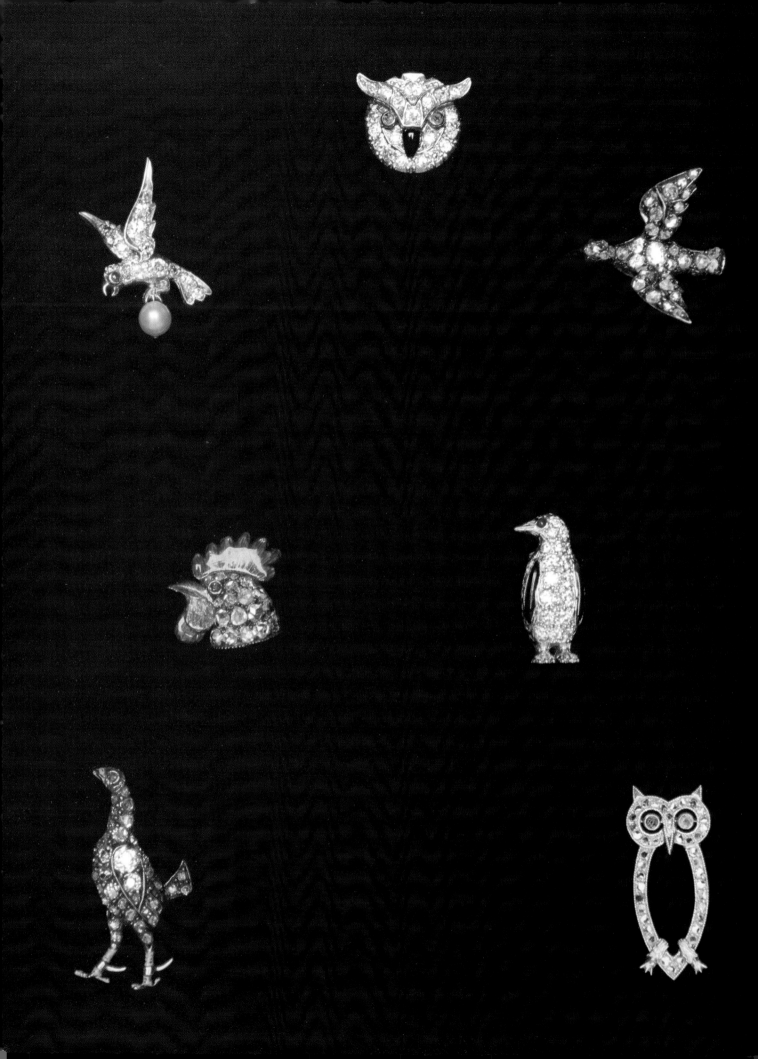

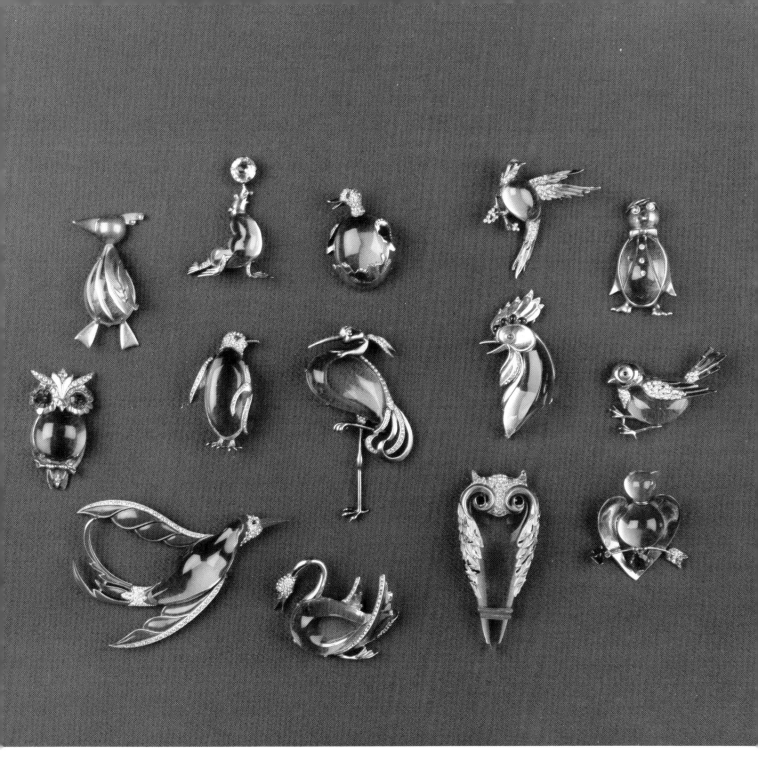

*Opposite page:*

**Antique scarf pins**

Owl's head of platinum of 14k. gold with 20 diamonds, two emerald eyes, and a sapphire beak, French. / Hawk of platinum and 14k. gold with 15 diamonds, a ruby and a pearl, circa 1890. / Flying curlew (gull) of 14k. gold with 31 rose diamonds and ruby eyes, probably French, circa 1875. / Rooster's head of 14k. gold and silver with 18 rose diamonds and red enamel, French. / Penguin of platinum with 17 diamonds, onyx wings and a ruby eye. / Fighting cock of 14k. gold and silver 30 rose diamonds, six cut diamonds, English, circa 1870. / Owl of platinum and 14k. gold with four old rose diamonds and emerald eyes, French. Private collection through Leonard D. Prins. $1250-2250 each.

**Birds with clear bellies**

Each of these wonderful brooches has clear Lucite as a central component of its design, circa 1945. Trifari made the stork, duck in an egg, rooster head, song bird, swan and penguin. Sandor made the big owl. Jolle made the bird with the heart. Corocraft made the enameled bird on a branch. The other brooches are not marked. Joan Rothstein Toborowsky. E. & J. Rothstein Antiques. $250-600 each.

**Victorian swallows**
Three fine brooches designed as swallows, each pavé-set with diamonds, circa 1860.
N. Bloom & Son. Left $1500-1800, center $3800-4000, right $1000-1200.

**Charming waterfowl**
Gold pendants of birds common to water habitats are carefully crafted in these designs of the 1980s. Beebe Hopper. $175-550.

**A forest scene**
Osprey brooch of 9k. pink, white and yellow gold with enamel, $1200-1500. / Squirrel and branch brooch of white, pink and yellow gold, $600-700. / Two songbirds of 18k. gold with nephrite leaves and coral berries, Swedish, made in 1952, $1850-2250. / Bee brooch set with rubies and diamonds, $1250-1500. N. Bloom & Son.

**A humm-dinger**
Gold hummingbird brooch set with a marquise ruby eye, pavé diamond head, carved sapphire chest, and body set with sapphires perched on a gold branch with carved sapphire, ruby, and turquoise leaves, circa 1950. Sandy DeMaio. $6500-8000.

**Pretty Polly**
Parrot brooch of rectangular and asymmetrical shaped stepout citrines and a diamond collet eye. Phillips Action. $1500-1800.

**My heart took flight**
Antique brooch with a deep purple amethyst of heart shape, gold, pearl and diamonds, circa 1880. N. Bloom & Son. $900-1200.

**Proud and exotic**
Peacock brooch of two-colored gold, the cascading plumes set with sapphires, the wings and breast with graduated sapphires and emeralds, all mounted on a branch with seven marquise diamond leaves, circa 1960. Phillips Auction, $6800-8250.

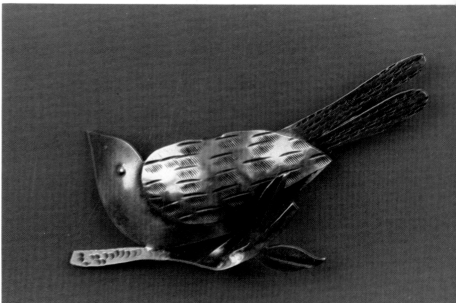

**Silver wings**
Sterling silver bird brooch by Rebajez, circa 1950. Muriel Karasik. $300-400.

# Index

**Shimmering grace**
Victorian brooch of five graduated diamond swallows *en trembant* and detachable. N. Bloom & Son. $18,000-20,000.